LET ME LOVE MYSELF

KIKI TSIRIDOU

BALBOA.PRESS
A DIVISION OF HAY HOUSE

Balboa Press books may be ordered through booksellers or by contacting:

Balboa Press
A Division of Hay House
1663 Liberty Drive
Bloomington, IN 47403
www.balboapress.com
844-682-1282

Cover layout designed by Vrochidou Panagiota

Print information available on the last page.

ISBN: 978-1-9822-7858-8 (sc)
ISBN: 978-1-9822-7859-5 (e)

Balboa Press rev. date: 01/21/2022

To Dimitrios, for his everything! His great light has helped me find my own. To my kids Vaios and Efterpi who make me feel blessed every single day.

Contents

Acknowledgement

I would like to thank my family for all their support and faith in me. They were my driving force to complete this work with all their love surrounding me. Every step I made they were there to ensure me that I head towards the right direction of inner peace and love.

My special thanks to my master of mind, Anthimos, who shared all this knowledge with me, who believed in me and led me to the path of my inner light. His help to my transformation was a divine present for me.

Last but not least, I have to admit that no person came to my way without a reason. Whether they intended to enlighten me or not, I consider them part of my life and feel blessed.

Introduction

Welcome to the most exciting, challenging self improving journey. Our destination is all the wealth and light we hide either because of being unaware or due to our lack of trust and love to ourselves. This book is written with the unique target to move you discover your inner treasure and free you of all the misunderstood beliefs that keep you chained to the acceptance that your fate has not been very generous with you. This book sheds light on your path of redemption and leads you to your inner treasure. Your inner discovery will lead you appreciate yourself, your life and feel blessed you are a part of this world. This analytical step by step guide brings you closer to your reality and gratitude so that you discover yourself and not avoid your real entity.

It is time we learnt ourselves! Time we loved ourselves! Such a big promise we owe to give us in order to find inner peace and live our lives to the full. Just think how social conventions have misdirected our inner freedom. We iron our clothes, we do everything to have and show a smooth face but we choose to crumple our soul. Let's wonder why we do that to ourselves and how I can take my fulfilling life in my hands! Is it better to struggle to be more likeable to all others than love myself?

Of course we live in a society and man has been a social being for time immemorial! Of course we need family, friends, and colleagues around us, next to us but not above us. The point is to be what we really are and not what others want us to be. If we try to change and adjust to what others approve of us without respecting our inner being, then many problems will start emerging such as anger, illness, unhappiness, misery and we keep a distance from loving ourselves.

This book has been written in order to help you get rid of everything others have put on you in order you become they way they want you to be. It is not fair to live your whole life in your body, which does not include only your physical body, but your aura, your sentimental and mental body too, and not get to know you, respect you, and love you! How unfair it is to disrespect your inner strengths and powers just because others can't stand your uniqueness!

Society would be a better place if we listened to our inner voice, learnt to understand the signs our unconscious mind sends us and expressed our inner energy. Everyone was born to do a different job for the evolution of humanity and we have to respect this. Everyone is different and we need to understand this. Everyone follows a different way and we need to realize this. Everyone offers in a different way to evolution and we need to appreciate it! Everyone is a whole small universe and we need to follow its rules!

When I say to respect our soul I don't mean to disrespect others. Inner evolution has nothing to do with others. If I realize who I am, what my strengths are, the reason I was born, how to express my soul, I have no reason to be unkind or hard on others. Of course, my universe is not the only one that exists! Everyone has his own sun and orbit and we must respect all the cosmic laws in order to live in harmony and not crash. If everyone got to know themselves, they would not feel victims, unloved or angry, and inner peace and love would take the steering wheel leading humanity to a better place.

Let's try to analyze why it is so difficult to discern our own needs from what social conventions need. Why we choose to unhappy in order to keep others pleased. Why it is so difficult to realize that everyone can be contented and balanced as long as we are faithful to our real selves.

Inner peace is not something that is limited or shared. There is enough for everyone! If you are happy, it does not mean that you took my share and there is not enough for others. If you find your inner purpose of life, it does not mean that I have to lose mine. Everyone has their own share and the most difficult thing is to discover it.

Deficiency is innate

Let's start with deficiency. Let's discover the reason we feel stressed and unhappy if we don't have what others have. Here, we fall into the trap of focusing on what we lack and not what we have. Being ungrateful is the greatest sin for me because we take for granted everything we have and direct our thoughts to what we do not possess. If we think deeper, everything we struggle to acquire is of material nature such as a new fast car, a bigger house, new clothes, whatever has to do with perishable acquisitions. We are led to forget and not realize that everything that makes us complete and happy, is inside us. Let's start discovering the journey that leads to our inner inclusiveness and wholeness!

We were born on this planet and the axis of the earth has an inclination of 23 degrees towards its revolving axis. This makes it move in an elliptical orbit. Consequently, we were born on an elliptical planet and it is a natural law that we will always lack something. There will always be something missing from our lives. This should become a fact and not an elusive purpose.

It is worth wondering why instead of wasting our vital energy, thoughts and power to fight in order to acquire what we lack, we still can't get used to this fact, accept it, and live in harmony with this natural law that governs this planet for thousands of centuries. What is the reason our mind goes directly to inadequacies, instead of enjoying the countless gifts we were given?

It is all a matter of energy direction. Energy has existed on this planet for millions of years. Only when energy was directed through the cable, were we able to enjoy the benefits of electricity. The same rule applies to us. Only when we direct our energy towards the right direction will we be able to enjoy the benefits which will enlighten our lives. If our cable is full of holes, our energy will be wasted without producing light. In other words, if we focus on what is missing from our lives and chase phantoms, we can't make full use of our powers and finding peace and our purpose is a midnight dream.

It is such a shame to spend a whole life in misery just because we do not have something, while inside me, a whole world of powers, talents, skills remain locked. It is unfair for ourselves to use the key of our hearts trying to unlock the wrong doors. Our heart and soul always show us the way. We need to keep calm and listen to your inner voice calling us.

Reasons we experience deficiency in a painful way

Let's take things from the beginning. Before we were born, in the belly of our mothers, we experienced full wholeness. In our first and unique experience on this planet, we were given everything we needed, before even asking for them. We lived in our paradise. No external fact could influence us. Cold or heat, a sunny or a cloudy day, a cheerful or a mean neighbor, could not affect our mood.

All these experiences are locked in a black box, very well hidden in our subconscious, but the key is missing. The paradox is that these experiences have the power to influence us to a greater extent than we can imagine.

From the first moment of our birth, lack of something starts. We are cold, hot, thirsty and hungry; we feel lack of security, lack of love, lack of material things. The child must cry in order to ask others to cover their basic needs. This comes to full opposition to the previous living conditions, where the ultimate coverage of our needs prevailed and was taken for granted. We were thrown out of our paradise but we still can't realize that we are a small universe and have to find our own orbit and not stumble on orbits of other universes. It is strange, though, that as we grow older and realize what happens, we are stubbornly stuck to the embryonic phase and continue complaining for things we do not have until we die instead of working towards standing on our own feet.

We see many people being so attached to the past that their discussions, their thoughts and their practices concern mainly the past. They have forgotten the hard times and remember only those good old days. It is alright with that as long as we don't refuse to walk forwards. We evolve only by looking ahead. The loss we experience with our birth still chases our present. Our work should focus on how to overcome painful situations and try to exploit our dynamic power inside us instead of being stagnant to the past. The same rule applies with memories that are painful to remember. The solution here is to stop and think what this painful experience has to teach me. If we think even deeper, the body of ours that is affected, is our sentimental one, and if don't overcome it in time, it is going to show its effects and pain on our physical body too.

Now, it is our chance to understand that this loss, this pain, this hardship was our freedom. Our defeat is our teacher. Let's remember the lesson and forget pain. How else can we learn? If we realize how many times we fall over until we learn to walk, we will see that it is not so terrible. Nobody would like to have a mum telling us that we must stop trying to stand up and walk because we are going to fall over and hurt our knees. We would still be in bed! I am sure you can't even imagine it. I am also sure that it used to be more painful than what we are going through.

Through the lack we experience, we have been stuck to the idea that every deficiency is terrible. We tend to long for things we don't have and we forget to admire or value the ones we have.

We must understand why feeling badly is easier that feeling happy. First of all, bad situations are easier to happen. Take a relationship for example. It takes two to start a relation but it only takes the will of one to break up. The feeling that we cannot predict a difficult situation makes us anxious. This is because we cannot realize that this unpredictable situation which hurts us is on our way. We must overcome it and get out of it wiser than when we entered.

In addition, fear has existed since people lived in caves. It comes from our archetypes. The period we had to fight with wild animals. The utopia is that fear still exists. But now, I live in a house not a cave. Fear is the child of our mind. It has occupied a very comfortable seat in the middle of our minds and it resists being dethroned. Nobody wants to lose his comfort and authorization; likewise fear will always try not to lose its prominent position on your mind.

We need to understand the mechanism and start thinking of the positive side of uncomfortable events so that fear gets the message that there is the possibility of being replaced with a positive feeling. In order to achieve this, we must work towards it and start sending the message to our brains that fear is unwanted. Bit by bit, we will see that the message has been received.

Understanding negativity

It is time everyone showed our power. It is time we understood the utopia of our problems. Who persuaded me that the purpose of live is marriage? Who planted the belief that money is the only key to happiness on my mind? Who defined that the only way to be respectable is a high salary and an expensive car? The most certain thing is that we were not born with these beliefs.

Only if we realize that all my problems stem from the past, and all our anxieties concern the future, will we be able to understand that we lose the present. What's the point of worrying about things that are over, or things that may never happen? We expect our life to belong to the present, and we do exactly the opposite. Time is not linear but circular. That's why we may realize that our life makes circles. Just like the planets. Time is infinite moments of the present. Every moment of the present is a new now. Only when we are able to enjoy every moment of now, will we get rid of fear, anger, and guilt! Don't forget that others taught you to feel this way; it is their planted thought on your mind. What we have to realize is that we have hard times because others put problems on our way. We try to solve problems that are not ours.

It often happens to go to the cinema with my friends and think of the clothes I have to wash the next day. As a result I miss valuable moments of relaxation. There is no way to enjoy tender moments with my partner when I think of the office appointments scheduled for next day. Once again I miss moments that could accompany me for the whole day. All this is my choice, but nobody taught me to undertake my responsibilities. It is easier to put the blame on my life, job, boss, Jupiter. Unchain your mind and fully consciously enjoy every moment of now to the full. That's why it is called present. Every moment of present is a unique present. You always have the option to choose what to enjoy and what to let upset you. Remember that seat on your brain that waits for happiness to sit.

If every choice of yours is the voice of your inner soul, then it is a matter of time to dethrone fear and stress, giving the seat to happiness and optimism. It is up to you. It takes rehearsals over and over again until you achieve it. It is the same mechanism as everything else we learn. In order to learn music it needs rehearsals, in order to learn how to build a wall it takes time, in order to learn how to write it takes years. How else can you learn? The same rule applies to everything.

Can you think of the internal meaning of it? In order a poet to write a poem he needs to know how to write, but not all people who know how to write can write inspired poems. It is up to our passion, will and hard work. Whoever wants to reach a destination, a first step and the stamina to proceed is necessary.

Another way to fight the misery of deficiency is to adapt to the conditions I meet on my way. Think of dinosaurs. They were the conquerors of this planet, but they have disappeared when they could not adapt to new conditions. Man is not the strongest creature, neither does he fly higher, nor jumps longer. What saves him is the ability to adapt to new environment by using his brain and his will to survive.

Let's try to apply this fact to our everyday lives. Let's adjust ourselves with or without money, in cold or hot weather, married or single, and so on. We must not forget that evolution requires changes. Every change has something to teach us. Let's stick on the lesson and not the pain. Let's stop thinking over and over again the things we are deprived of. There is no need to be deprived of the joy of my soul to adapt to new conditions, new experiences, new chances, just because I don't want to change my routine. And they ought to change. If things did not change, we would still live in caves.

Try, for example, to hold a piece of paper which is as light as feather. It looks easy. After some time, your arm will start hurting you. The paper is not heavier but your arm is hurting you more and more. You have the option of remaining in the same position or alter it by changing the hand that holds the paper. You have the option of suffering from tendinitis or achieve your goal. The whole trial is just to teach you that when you are hurt, change stance. It is so simple and it is a pity to see people to refuse to change and adapt to new situations. Why does pain attract us and we believe that this is the right situation?

Who taught you that life is a painful procedure? Who told you that life is full of hardships and problems we have to suffer without being able to overcome them? Who told you that this is our destiny? Who taught you that every difficult situation must throw you in a swampland and there is no way out? The only certain thing is that you were not born with these beliefs. If we start realizing that all these problems are our teachers in order to be wiser and stronger then we would welcome them and we would be able to see the collateral beauty. They are the lesson we had to learn as we had misunderstood something. They are our guides to show us that someone else has put his psychological state on us.

I admit it is not easy to adapt to new data. But you have to, if you want to survive. Joy will come. It is waiting just outside the door. You only have to decide to open the door and welcome it. Stop looking back at the past, and don't think of tomorrow. Whoever created you, wants you happy. Pain is the way to reach your destination. It is the lesson you have to study. Pain is the procedure to walk along the long twisted road in order to reach the top.

A good way to stop negative thinking is, every time that an uncomfortable thought crosses your mind, immediately turn it into something positive. For instance, don't say that you don't have enough money for a bigger house. Instead, you can say that you get by perfectly now. Don't say I find my job boring, but be thankful you have a job. Don't think of perfect bodies; think that your body can carry you wherever you want. Don't feel unhappy because your eyes are not blue; feel grateful that your eyes allow you to see. Stop thinking that you are not happy enough, but feel safe and resilient you are alive with thousands of opportunities open up in front of you, waiting from you to open the eyes of your soul to experience them. With persistence and hard work everything you want to achieve is feasible.

All in all, be thankful and grateful for all you have. Think of how many millions of people out there wish to have what you don't appreciate, what you have and take it for granted. Never forget that no significant feat was easy. Don't stick to the problems. Discover your inner strength, your own will, your own goals, your own destination, listen to your own soul, your own inner voice and go get them.

Let's open our eyes, admire the infinite blue of the sky and inhale the gift of living the present. Feel blessed you have the chance to do things to help humanity any way you can. Everyone is necessary on this planet. There are not good or bad jobs. This is the game of the society. It is the trap. Follow your own way and think that dead fish follow the tide. You have to realize that you have everything needed to create your own way. It does not matter if others don't approve of it just because they can't feel or understand it. We all go to the same destination, but we don't follow the same way. Everyone has to place his own little stone in order to build the big feat of humanity.

Be sure to have placed your own little stone there. Be part of this world and not an observer. Suppose that you are sitting on the bleaches of a stadium watching athletes to train. It seems easy to judge or criticize their performance. Their training looks even easier. I can give them advice or shout at them when their record is not the desired or the expected one. When I get into the truck I will understand that it is not easy but hard work is the key to success. Don't be afraid to get into the truck of your own life, break your own record, and get the great satisfaction of success.

The more you try the better results you are going to have. But try. Stop watching life passing in front of you. Be part of it. Be part of the team of humanity and help as much as you can. Do it with all your heart and you will see that negativity will be thrown out of your mind. Your happiness levels are going to rise significantly and you are going to feel that life is a present. Happiness comes when we have tried hard and achieved things we have chosen.

Anger

Have you ever thought why we get angry? Why do we feel upset? What fuels this negative feeling? Is there a way not to allow some situations or people to affect our life? Let's untangle the truth and see the reasons we chose to afflict our mental health.

Many people think they are deceived; their good heart is to blame as others do not appreciate their help or others underestimate them and this makes them stop moving. All these feelings come to your brain just to make you feel a victim, start complaining while feeling you can do nothing to avert the situation.

The awareness of the situation is half the way to our salvation. The longer you keep your anger inside you, the more time you lose, the more energy you waste and the more you torture yourself. It is a matter of time to reach a point you focus on every negative and troubled state that there is no room in your mind for positive thoughts and worthwhile experiences. It's no wondering the same adverse and gloomy thoughts flood our head over and over again. Not only do we allow our energy to be wasted and feel weaker and sadder, but also we feel that there is no way out.

The key point is to realize what anger is. It is a fire that burns in your chest. The longer we keep flames lit inside us, the greater part of you it is going to destroy. The dilemma you face is, if you let it out, you are going to burn others; on the other hand, if you keep it hidden in the inner part of you, it is going to burn your soul. You start feeling stressed not knowing what to do. Have you ever realized that it is not a lose - lose situation? Either odds or even, you are a loser. And the choice is yours. You actually know that it is really unimaginable that whatever course of action you adopt, it leads you to distress and misery.

It goes without saying that you think of others' reaction. You do not want to spoil your perfect image. If we think deeper, we are going to realize that our image is more important than our soul. Why should I care to such a destructive extent about what others think of me? And here I ask you! Is it possible to be likeable to everyone? Does it serve any purpose? What makes me happier? Do I love myself or wait for others to love me? Do I admire my qualities or leave it to the taste of others to admire me. Do I choose to get to know who I am and respect myself or expect others to discover my inner beauty? You can easily realize that this leads you to a dead end. You have to transmit the message to every cell of your body that you love them, you respect them and you are their leader not their enemy.

The longer it takes us to realize it, the longer we put the blame on any external factor, just to cover our own weakness. For example many people's mood depends on the weather. They have headaches when it is cloudy, they are in a bad mood when it is rainy and when summer comes they can't stand heat. How logical is it to bet bottom dollar on the weather, your rude neighbor, or the retrograde motion of Hermes. An external circumstance deprives you of the ability to stand on your feet and feel happy. Have you ever looked deeper inside you and wondered if it is their fault or yours that let them affect your inner balance and happiness? Why do you choose to let others drive your soul's vehicle? Why do we let others choose the way we are going to follow?

It is an undeniable fact that we were not born with the self serving objective to feel ill- disposed. It only takes conscience to conceive that *you* are the only one responsible for this uncomfortable state. It needs work to take up the driver's seat. The vehicle is yours and it is the best gift you have ever been given.

Fighting aggression

The key to fight anger is to comprehend that every difficult situation brings you before two doors. You have two choices. The realization you have to make is that whichever door you choose to enter is a decision which should be taken fully consciously with self- knowledge so as not to feel sorry for the choice you have rejected. It is important not to have second thoughts. In any case you feel discomfort, you have to recognize what is the reason you did not act according to your will. You should identify the reason why you did not hear what your soul had to tell you and you didn't decide fully consciously so that the other option had been fully rejected. What is that you misunderstood?

Taking a decision with full conscience means you are the leader of your life. You head towards the right direction and you don't expect any third factor to tell you the way. Now, you will feel contented either it is cold or hot, whether your neighbor is in a good or a bad mood. You do not need anyone else to define and to confirm the great entity you are. There is no point in looking in your mirror and see yourself through the eyes of others. Be yourself! Act yourself! Express yourself! Love yourself! And only *you* can achieve this. If you do not devote time, work and thought to turn on your innate bright light, why should others bother? This is your big ego that has wrapped you up and prevents you from moving on.

Knowing yourself will enable you to release yourself from the stress to keep everyone happy and satisfied, paying the toll of mistreating yourself. When you are authentic, your relations are clarified and you are not pressed to prove something else beyond what you really are. Get rid of all the fixed beliefs that your purpose in life is making others happy. If you are contented and joyful, others will be too, but first don't forget to be delightful with your real self, the one you see with the eyes of your soul.

All the great philosophers talked about knowing thyself and it constitutes the gigantic value of being loyal to your soul and your inner self. Only then will you enjoy the present called life to the full. How can I expect from a body and a soul I do not respect, to function well? Would you do your best in favor of somebody who mistreats you? Why should your body do it for you? Who do you think you are? Again your big ego came to the scene. So, starting understanding yourself will lead to loving yourself unconditionally and the gratitude of your inners self will become evident very soon. It is an action and reaction relationship. It is up to you to realize and respect this law. The law exists! It depends on you if you accept and use it or disrespect and suffer.

Never forget that we are energy. Otherwise what's the point of using a defibrillator which delivers electric shocks via wires to bring heartbeats back to normal? Without energy, nothing works. Think of a simple clock. The hands of the clock won't move. Stop having the misconception that you are all-powerful. Saving energy will help you have the power to know, accept and love yourself. Be a conductor of your energy and make room to gather even more so that it does not burn you but be sufficient to light your inner light. Be ready to discover your inner sun. Do not be afraid to be bright and light up. You owe it to your Creator and your soul. The general belief that everything goes wrong does not concern you. This is for those who choose to feel this way. Not for you. You have a hidden light that waits from you to be used. If you manage to reveal it, others will see it too and this way you help others too by showing them the right and bright way to love themselves.

Let me give you an example of how anger has the power to force you to lose vital energy. Suppose you have the indicative amount of energy of 100Watt when you start your day. On your way to work, you have a quarrel with someone over a parking space. He shouts at you, you feel insulted and you think that the only way out of this situation is to talk back in an impolite way. You feel disgraced and your aura has been filled with negativism. You have already lost 10 Watt and you are left with 90. This happened because you would never let another ego get higher than yours. When you are at work, you can't make full use of your abilities, you are nervous and your performance is deficient. After 8 hours of frustration, you feel that today is not your day, because you have already lost another 10 Watt. Tiredness starts appearing. You can't wait for the time to go home and relax. The headache has already been sensed. When you get home, the first thing you see is whatever is not at its place, whatever gives you a reason to complain. This might be a pair of slippers out of the shoe organizer or dirty glasses in the sink. You start shouting, feeling unappreciated and you see your family members as enemies. The argument is only moments away. You probably yell, cry, and feel underestimated and betrayed. Have you realized that you are left with 70 Watt? After all that, undoubtedly, you don't feel like watching your favorite series or enjoy a glass of wine. You go to bed feeling nervous, upset with the belief that everything goes wrong. The bright side of life has been excluded from your frame of mind. After all these thoughts that unconsciously have occupied the most comfortable seat of your mind, it is most definitely that you can't sleep well. Your night sleep is not calm and your body does not get the rest it deserves in compensation of its hard work to serve you all day. You are being ungrateful to your body and the millions of cells that work hard for your being healthy. When you wake up, you feel exhausted and your getting ready for work suddenly looks boring and tiresome. Negative thoughts find the entrance door open to enter. Pessimism has just intruded and it is you that have welcomed it. That's natural because you have only 60 Watt left.

And it's time I asked you, whose fault is it? Who allowed this to happen? You don't have to try hard to recognize yourself. Only you are responsible for letting all this energy loss take place. And the most disappointing realization is that the one who lacks high energy levels is you! Do you get the idea that you yourself harmed your mental and physical health? May I ask you how often do you let this happen to yourself? And the obvious question arises: Don't you love yourself?

It is quite weird to think what we do to ourselves. We abuse us and behave in the harshest way we would never dare maltreat anyone else. If somebody harmed you and beat you up in such a brutal way, how long would you help and be at his service? Definitely not for long. And why should your body continue to appreciate you? I am sorry to say that revenge is on the way! And it is the right reaction because it is you who acts and your body reacts. You act with your sentimental thoughts and your mind reacts too.

It stands a good reason to pop the query how to avoid energy loss. Well, Christ spoke with parables and when He said "if anyone slaps you on the right cheek, turn to him the other also" He was talking about energy. Let's see the connection with our example. If you never let the argument with the other driver happen, and even if he insulted you, you were apathetic with no need to attract all the negativity, you wouldn't lose a day or two of your life feeling upset and quarrelsome. If you were ready to laugh at his disrespect you would have kept your 100Watt and you could have taken another 10 from him. That would make you have 110 Watt which meant that you could give the extra 10 Watt to someone else. Yes, you wasted your love energy, just for nothing. You fell into the trap of your big ego. It is egoistic to act as if am the centre of the whole universe. Always bear in mind that you are the centre of your universe, but never forget that others have their own universe too. Do not try to impose your orbit entangle with other orbits. Think of the universe! Think of all harmonious revolving that does not let collision with others. They follow the rules. And we should learn from these rules. They are our teachers to free us from being egoists.

There is no other way to approach the reality of the mechanism that moves everything around us but to see the analogy from greater parts to smaller parts which are inside us. Open your eyes, your thoughts, be receptive to knowledge offered to you from greater beings in order to connect knowledge and follow what they have been trying to teach us for millions of years now. It does not require special skills, just work, love and the strength to free ourselves of our big ego.

Egoism

Egoism is of major importance and hard work should start from the question why we choose to abuse our body and soul. Why do we prefer to be victims instead of winners? Undoubtedly, it's not easy to realize that our ego has grown bigger than it deserves. Egoism has occupied a big part of us and in no way is it willing to move. Will we leave it there conquer our life? Of course not. What do we do to remove it from the center of our soul? Nothing! Here is the paradox!. Our life is full of two – pole conditions, beliefs, conclusions, feelings, opinions, ways of thinking and the list goes on. We choose nagging instead of smiling, feeling hopeless than hopeful, misery than happiness, jealousy than gratitude, ugliness that the beauty of our souls.

Isn't it a pity to have been given a wonderful gift and do whatever you can to destroy it? Would you do that to a sofa? A porcelain vase? A plasma TV set? Surely not. Why do we do that to ourselves? Do we love more the sofa than our souls? Do we value more the vase than our inner euphoria? Do we respect a TV set more than ourselves? Of course not. Then what or who prevents you from feeling comfortable and delightful with the unique present you are gifted?

Our ego places us to the centre of everything. We think that we deserve the most, we are the best, we are the only blessed creature on this planet, we know everything, we can judge and criticize everyone, we are on top of everyone. This great disrespect to the fact that we are a part of this cosmic existence and everything and everyone has a share and a role to play is fed by our ego. We are unique and different but not the only ones.

I have to admit that it is quite complicated to understand how our body works. Stop and think that you do not know the way a TV set works too, but you take care of it. If you start taking care of yourself too, your cells will understand it and they will update their functions. Trust and love them. They are not ungrateful. They just seek the harmonious function in order to keep you healthy and contented. So, start loving you now! Do not waste another minute of really living and savoring the real taste of life.

We choose the role of being victims

I am sure that all of us want to be the masters of our body and soul. On the other hand, every time someone tells us a problem he faces, or a difficult situation he experiences, we try to prove him that we are in a more adverse position. We automatically feel the need to confirm that our problem is far greater. Why does this happen? What force have we allowed to take over and drive my vehicle? Why are we afraid to accept we feel happy and blessed? Young children show their happiness and shout out their joy as loud they can. No kid can hide his enthusiasm and fervor. What has changed since then? Who stole my innocence? Who I gave permission to make me think that misery is the way we should feel? Are feelings one size? What keeps us from feeling blessed about what we have? Why do we believe we are superior to the many millions of people who are struggling and praying for what we have? But instead of being contented and divine we just feed our ego by complaining and grumbling.

It is up to you to change this. Yes, the work should be done by you. Now it is the time you undertook the responsibility, the responsibility that concerns you and only you. This is the hardest point because there is nobody else to blame or do it for you. Now, it is time you took on the responsibility for yourself. The time of facing responsibility is the greatest moment to free you. Nobody likes responsibilities or at least this was what you were led to believe. I am sure you cannot even remember who passed this belief on you. Real free people do not fear to mask their faults or strengths. Real free people love the way they are. Love to be themselves. The moment you realize that your freedom is up to you, then the whole universe is open up to help you. The only thing you have to do is raising your head and keep your eyes open looking deeply in your inner self.

The oddity we go on following is that it is not right to do something wrong. We think of ourselves as Mr. Perfects. I am sure you know now who has entered the cracks you have forgotten unlock. It is an old acquaintance of yours, named Big Ego. If you don't throw it away right now, it will try to direct your thoughts. And remember it is only you that lets it take the steering wheel of your life. This way, it acquires the necessary strength to give you a ride to wherever direction it serves it to lead you.

Your words are heard

How often do you hear yourself saying: "It is the society's fault", "that's my fate", "I was born to suffer" or "the only thing I can do, is being patient"? If you jump to such wrongly believed conclusions easily, stop and think! Are you aware that every single word we say has a certain vibration? Every aspect of our life is under certain laws in accord with physics or natural laws. Have you already forgotten that it's all a matter of action and reaction? You get whatever you ask for.

If every morning you start your day by saying "I feel bored", "I don't like my job", "Nobody loves me" "I don't like my life", do you think your angel, creator, energy, destiny, say it as you like, will give you something different ? It will give you exactly what your words vibrated. What you asked for is a boring job, nobody to love you, and an unhappy life. This is what was heard. Why should it bring you something different? If you ask me for a spoonful of sugar why should I give you a bowl of lentil soup? Holly books tell it: Ask, and it will be given to you. The law does its job and it is exclusively your choice to follow it or not. If your ego makes you question it, it is not the law's problem. The problem is entirely yours.

You can realize now the wrong way we have taken. But there is a turning point just in front of you. Break it and change direction. You control your life. You were born to be happy. The vehicle you drive is all yours and you deserve it. Now it is time you learnt to fill it with the right kind of fuel. The fuel that keeps your engine in a perfect condition and prolongs its life spam is in your possession. The same way you ask for the best quality of goods, ask for the best beams universe can give you. You are a part of the universe and you deserve it. You can have everything you ask for as long as there is enough room inside you. Now, you may need to throw away all the previously false beliefs in order to make room for the newcomers. It works the same way with the old sofa. If you don't throw the old one, there is no room in your living room for a new one.

We must be really careful of what we say. It is heard and done. Don't be of the opinion that it is hard to change. It just takes faith and willingness. Bear in mind that when there is a will there is a way. It is of crucial importance to start thinking in a positive way. Get rid of negative thoughts. Feel glorified for everything you have. Stop feeling unappreciated. You are a valuable present to humanity. You are here to offer your divine energy to evolution. Progress needs and waits for your contribution. Don't forget that. Never allow a day to pass without feeling thankful for your life, your body, your inner strength.

If you knew the strength negative thoughts have on you and the way they come back to you due to the law action and reaction, you would stop using them from now on. You would delete them not only from your vocabulary but from your memory as well. It is easier to understand it if you think of the way echo sounds. Suppose you are at a spot in the mountains and you shout a word. After a while, this word will be heard back. There is no way of shouting a word and hear another in return. Again the law of action and reaction is in front of us and you will come face to face with it until it becomes a part of your brain and soul. Until then, keep your eyes open and observe how everything works.

If it is your conscious wish that chooses to live under fury and anger, it's ok. It's your choice. But ask yourself "why". However, if you embrace joy, happiness, blessing, creation, intense harmonious feelings, if you realize that every difficulty is the way to learn to stop agonizing, stop worrying, then it is a piece of cake to change your way of thinking. It only takes harmlessness and the driving force of love. If you never forget that you were not born to suffer, then you are ready to start working towards your transformation. You are going to live appreciating every experience which made you a little bit wiser. Step by step.

Every time you feel hurt, think of the reason why you feel this way. Think of the lesson you have to learn. Even when we learn how to ride a bike, we fall off. What does it mean? Never ride a bike again? Of course not. It is a lesson for you to learn that you should be more careful and look in front of you. The way your eyes are formed wants to tell you something. Look straight ahead. The eyes of birds are different. They need to look sidewise. This protects them. You are protected by looking in front of you and not be polarized and go off your course by looking to your left or right. The sun gives us another bright example. It follows the right direction without going to the north or to the south. Why do you prevent your own sun from expressing its brightness?

As you work towards the right orientation, you are going to see things from another perspective. The positive one. You are going to start realizing that every problem has something to tell you. Every obstacle has something to show you, as long as you have your eyes wide open to see the message, free from your big ego. So, next time you think that hardships and destiny hit you without mercy, ask yourself what the lesson you have to learn is. This is the key to find the correct answers. Answers that will enlighten your inner soul provided that you try to connect your conscious with the unconscious mind and get rid of the dipoles that polarized your way of you think.

Let's give a very simple example. You say to your friend that you are going on a diet. You said it, you did not decide it consciously. You don't believe it! You just want to show you have the strength but behind on your mind doubts control your thoughts. This hidden message your doubts spread, is what is sent to the universe. Your second thoughts are already on the way. Deeply inside you, you know that you are not ready to go on a diet for a lot of reasons. You have already set a problem to yourself, which prevents you from doing it. Now you try to eat without being seen or you try to find an excuse in order to excuse yourself and not to show you are unreliable. Unreliable to whom? To others or yourself? What you have said has already led you to a situation you try to avoid. Who told you to do that? Try to understand that now you are in a worse position than before. Here you need your inner power to be consistent to yourself. Don't say it. Until, at least, you learn you can start being honest to you. You can tell your friend that you don't want to go on a diet and take the whole responsibility. If your friend tells you that you have no power over yourself, you can tell them that today you don't have the power, but you may have tomorrow.

In order to avoid this hit that hurts you, you do things worse. You hide it, you get up at night, and you try to explain that you didn't mean that. You will always try to find an excuse that will make you feel comfortable. You will do everything to prevent it from coming out to light.

While you progress and this inner journey of yours takes you further, you will see that whatever you say regardless it is true or a lie, it will try to happen. You have to be observant to see these changes in the way you perceive things. It is the vibration of your words. «In the beginning was the Word, and the Word was with God, and the Word was God». You have to believe that your words have so much power you cannot perceive. If you try to observe your words and the things that happen to your life, you will realize that they are fully aligned. In essence, your invocation has been sent and it is on the way to be lifted. The time you will see the result depends on your evolution. So, realizing what you say, because it happens, can help you evolve. It is up to you to change your life drastically to the better or to the worst.

The more you realize that what you say comes back to you, the more careful of what you say will be. Don't say negative things, they will happen. Don't be miserable about your life, it will happen. Don't say you don't like your life, it will happen. Don't say you don't have enough money, it will happen. You can say that you have enough for the time being. You will see that every time being, you will have enough. If you start being consciously happy of every moment of now, you will be happy every day.

Has it ever happened to you to tell your friend a lie because you don't want to talk to him? Instead of being honest to her and mainly your soul, your mind tries to find an excuse. You say for example that you have to go somewhere and you don't have time to talk to her. Your words have been heard. It is very possible that an incident will force you go out. You asked for it! Do it! Stay to the good part of your words or else take the whole responsibility. If you insist on telling lies to yourself and you don't do it, you will see that a superior power will force you do what you said as an excuse. You will see that your excuse will come before you. You asked for it, you gave the order and it was given to you. Your words return back. Nobody is against you. Only your inner self tries to unite with you. Give love to receive love because you are love.

This is the way to stop talking nonsense. You will understand that instead of telling lies and excuses, you can tell the truth as long as you are ready to take the responsibility. You could just say that you are not in the mood of talking to her more than three minutes. Why do you choose to tell lies to her? Why should you tell her that you have to go out? You have to understand that if you say so, you have to do so. You may as well tell her that you are not in the mood of talking to her. And the discussion stops there. If she loves and sympathizes with you, she will understand and she will not misunderstand or criticize you. She must respect the fact that you have a wish. Why should this wish be as she wants? Why should I disregard my need and accept hers? What makes it so difficult to tell the truth? Why do you need this great strength of power to express your feelings?

You have to explain to her clearly how you feel. If she is such an egoist as not to accept your wish, it's better not to call you again because she wants to impose her wish on you. To be precise she is a manipulative person. It needs guts to say that you don't want to talk to her now! And you should demand that she respect it. Of course, you will respect her wish in a similar situation. When she is not in the mood to pick up the phone and talk to you, you ought to respect it respectively with conscience. What is better than true communication without egoistic tendencies that hold you back?

Progress starts here. You do something for yourself and then for others. It is conscience that will help you go further. From the starting point you have reached the second step. On the third step you will see that what you say is done. Your lies become reality. That's right! Don't forget that you have said it. Don't stay in the excuse! To put it simple, live your life free of guilt. If you go further, you will see that the lie you told your friend becomes useful, as it will get you out of the house. It will force you to go out for a reason which will not please you. This way you will learn not to tell lies and do what your soul needs without building barriers. The only thing your soul asks from you is to please yourself, to respect yourself to love yourself. If you refuse to do what pleases you and do what pleases others, I am not my friend but your mum. And you have had enough for many years. Now, you are a grown up and you have to be aligned with your soul.

Moving on

It is time you stopped thinking about good and bad things. What is good for you may discommodes someone else or the other way round. We tend to believe that whatever puts us out of our regularity is bad. No, this has to change and look deeper inside you to see what this belief has to tell you. When you understand it, just change it. It is that simple. Take the turning, or hold the piece of paper with your other hand. The answer seeks your internal sun to shine. Do not block it. The only one who is going to suffer and feel distressed is you. It is like learning how to write. They have showed you a certain way to form the letters when you were young, but when you formed your personality, you gave them the direction, formation, speed that is expressed from deep inside you. Everything operates under the same laws and connects everything around you to find the answers.

While moving towards you will appreciate life, start collecting energy, and become wiser. You will feel free from the narrow limits of misery and stop suffocating just because you can't handle pessimistic habits. It's all on your mind. Just change the tenant that has occupied your brain. Never forget that the brain is yours. Do not leave it to the taste of others.

You would never choose to allow someone who destroys your property to rent it, why then allow negativism destroy your mind? Another oddity that never crossed your mind, respectively, is that you dust your furniture but you choose to praise the dust of your brain and you don't get rid of it. You choose to be likeable to others and be hostile with yourself. It sounds weird and the paradox is that you have not even realized it. But, it is you that caused it, not others. Now you know, start cleaning it up.

It is time we looked at ourselves straight into the eyes of our soul. It is time we perceived the lesson we have to learn every time we are hurt. It is time we pushed negativism out of the throne of our mind. It is time we opened a new window, allowing fresh air and sunshine to enter. It is time everything that used to upset us stopped governing us.

Remember your parents when you were young, and you were about to go out, telling you "be careful" far more times than "enjoy yourself". Why give greater power to negativity and think that something bad is easier to happen than something good? Our brain is full of toxicity which we ourselves have offered it the throne in the middle of our brain. Then we start suffocating and the only way to breathe is to put the blame of responsibility to others. It is easier to blame someone else than myself because of that big ego we possess.

In many cases, it is our second nature to take the role of the victim. It is natural as it is the easiest role to play. There is no need to work towards a goal. I just throw the ball to the others. I put the blame on everyone and everything and I feel no remorse, I see no reason to feed my mind with healing thoughts. It is the easiest way as I only have to criticize a third person or factor. What I haven't realized is that this factor is beyond me. This is cheating. You may get the high grade but you will never learn the lesson.

I just apportion the responsibility of my own weaknesses on someone else. Why not, as long as I feel safe and comfortable? Ponder over it. How safe is it to allow the balance of my life and soul to others' hands? How comfortable is allowing others to determine my disposition? It is safer of course if I do not have the knowledge to do it on my own or if I don't want to work towards it and take on responsible.

Instead of trying to find the root why I allowed all gloomy emotions to overwhelm me and regulate me, causing pain and heartache, my struggle turns to finding someone to accuse. Feeling protected means feeling secure with myself. Not my mate, my money or my property. Everything may be lost in seconds and then what? Start feeling depressed? Why? Ask your inner you why! Why can an expensive car make you feel secure? Is it your vanity or a standing ethic of your social class? Why do you feel hurt if a friend keeps a distance from you? Is it loneliness that I fear of or I had used to feeling falsely amiable? Why does a comfortable sunny house give me greater pleasure than a comfortable sunny soul? Is my big ego again in front of me?

Let's think deeper and decide consciously if all the material goods I crave for, make me feel safe or just socially acceptable. Do they offer me true happiness or is it a mind game to avert me from finding inner peace? Of course goods are necessary but the point is to be fully conscious when I decide what to buy and what need of mine they will cover.

Materialism and aging

Undoubtedly, we have earthed and crystallized our achievements, our status and our faith in ourselves compared to the money we have in our bank account. Those who really care about what their soul asks them to be expressed and harmonize with their earthly life are not many. All this frenzy of zeal to earn more and more, to show off my material power, leaving our souls unfed has led people transmit very strong negative vibrations to the cosmic energy.

Let's analyze a little further the happiness levels material goods provide you with. Many of us are of the opinion that a fast new car will make us the happiest people in the world. It will help me prove my inner power and look worthy of existing. The same applies to clothes, shoes, bags and so on. Why do they make me feel happy? How conscious is our choice to buy something? Is it really what I need or does it have any connection with others? Do I believe it is a safety valve to help me love myself more as I regard it a prestige measure, or is it the way others will appreciate me more?

If we buy an expensive luxurious car just because we admire those who own one, and mistakenly have in mind that this purchase will attract people of the opposite sex, or people we look up to, imagine how we will feel when this outcome doesn't come true! Will our happiness levels be the same as when we bought it, after one year or two? In addition, how many people would choose a partner because of a car? And most importantly, do we want our partner to love us, or our car? All these questions have to be answered before your purchase.

And as time goes by, your happiness levels decrease because the desirable outcomes never came up. Your dream begins to fade. You may start feeling depressed and miserable. But don't worry; a new model of your favorite manufacturer has already been launched at the market. And the circle goes on and on. You are trapped in a vain circle, like a twisted snake eating its tail. The so called ouroboros which comes from the Greek word "oura" meaning tail and the word "voros" meaning eating. The question is: Can happiness be found this way? Do I put my dynamism in wrong priorities and I am deprived of my mental calmness? What is the unconscious gap I want to fill by caring so much about my image?

A notable point here is that we judge others according to our beliefs. If, for example I am ashamed of having an older mobile model, this belief automatically forces me to criticize those who own mobiles that are out of fashion. We must learn to recognize that whatever we gossip about are our beliefs. We judge others by our standards. Let's think deeper and find out what stops me from looking at the inner side of things. Every aspect of our life, every science, every one of us has an inner side that our subconscious mind tries to hide. Our work must be focused on brightening it bit by bit.

Here we have to decide will all our heart. Do I want to be me or be what others want me to be? Many people's main aim is to acquire more and more money, as they strongly believe this is the purpose they were born. They do not follow a career of their choice, a career that fulfils them, a career that suits their personality, but they choose one according to social beliefs. A post that will make them respected in the eyes of others. They spend their whole lives trying to achieve goals that are out of their spectrum of their inner needs. They get married not out of love but according to the social status and image. A partner who will help them maintain or advance the image they dream to create is the most suitable for them. They do not allow their soul to show them the right way.

More specifically, they even make friends that will help them belong to an upper class, or may go on holiday to places where they will find future customers. When they get older they are astonished at how quickly years have passed. They have spent their whole life trying to be on an unstable top and now that they are old, they decide to live. Unfortunately, years have passed and opportunities are limited. They have lost valuable time. No matter how much money and real property they have, they may feel jealous of someone they used to underestimate due to his lower social class, because they see they enjoy their life to the full, due to their happy moments they have chosen to live with the wife they truly love, their kids, real friends and having a job they do enjoy and feel contented. Walking bare foot on grass or tasting a cake with your finger can be unforgettable experiences too. There are cases that those seeking their lost chances, by acting unconsciously, may try to have an affair with the other person's wife just to show off their false power. Hidden jealous is behind. Not with the other's wife, but for the other's happy life. The difference is that, one chose the exterior side of life while the other listened to his interior voice. One chose to be likeable to others, the other preferred being likeable to his soul.

You may hear them recall youth. They will ask God why they can't be young again. They recall memories from their teenage years. They don't realize that they used to be young. They had been given this present. They just did not appreciate it. Whose fault is it that you cared only for money and did not enjoy these carefree years? This is another application of living every present moment consciously and feeling blessed and grateful.

There is nothing wrong about being successful and rich of course. The point you must think about is how conscious you are when you make decisions, the toll you pay, and if what you try to achieve will make *you* or others happy?.

These are questions easy to reply but they seem difficult to apply. Take a deep breath! Feel the air passing through all your cells! Relax your body! Then, take another deep breath and relax your feelings! Take a third breath and relax your thoughts. Think who you are! Who you really are! Feel grateful for what you are! Love yourself! Feel the star dust in you and the power it gives you. Everything works perfectly out there, why not inside you?

While this introspection journey unfolds, you may think of the paradox beliefs you are used to having. Every choice we make is a fight between your conscious and unconscious part. Our choices should be completely consciously made and we should be fully aware of its consequences so as not to cause an internal fight. Every dilemma you face has two doors. Stop and think with all your heart which one you are going to open, use all your inner love and listen to what your soul has to tell you. The choice you make should be the one you have good reasons to follow, and the one that will not cause seconds thoughts and regrets as far as the second option is concerned. If your decision is taken consciously, you won't worry about the option you have excluded. The result will be less stress and less worry. A conscious choice will help you feel strong and balanced. Second thoughts make you unstable and vulnerable. This way, your battery will stabilize and gradually it will charge. You avoid additional loss of energy, tiredness and psychological fatigue.

Only by a mindful administration of our energy and conscious choices can we have full cognizance of the consequences so that we don't care for the other door. This way, we start putting our thoughts in order and avoid unconscious disorder that may cause health problems. There is no need to let our mood, our energy, our peace of mind swaying back and forth. It is unfair to our soul. Keeping our soul contented starts with knowing what we do and the reason we do it. Being conscious sets the first step to enjoy every moment we live, the corner stone of start loving me.

Every time you get angry, distressed or upset, start thinking consciously why this certain fact or person has such a huge effect on you. Which gap did you leave open and it managed to sneak in? How can I lock my gaps so as to feel essentially secure with myself? It is time I loved myself! There is no other way to balance your thoughts, beliefs, ethics, relationships, feelings and emotions.

Friends

Friends are a gift and real friendship is a mixture of love, sincerity, understanding, devotion and so many other words describing this sacred relation. Real friends are a blessing to our lives. I am going to insist on the meaning of real friendship. Who is a real friend? The ancient Greek Philosopher Pythagoras who inspired Plato and Aristotle, defined friendship with amicable numbers. It is a fantastic way to understand real friendship harmony. It is worth studying this theory. Unfortunately, we may never have had the chance to delve into the hidden, inner meaning of friendship. It is the inner side of things we mentioned above. Who do you call a friend? Someone you know for a long time? Someone who trusts you unconditionally? Someone who is always there for you to listen to your problems? The one who is always willing to accompany you for an outing? The one who always tells the best for you? Someone who will help you advance socially? We all agree that each one separately and all of them together describe a healthy and real friendship.

And everything goes well until a "bad" moment" comes and this relation is not as precious as it used to be. After some time our beloved friend is someone we avoid being in the same room? He has become the person who betrayed your feelings, the one who took advantage of us and did not appreciate our good heart. You feel betrayed and disappointed. How come and the true feelings touch the other end of the pole and from best friends you approach the limits of sworn enemies?

Let's be more analytical. In the case you are willing to give the whole of you, what's the response of your friend? Does he appreciate it or does he take advantage of it? Does he need it or he just accepts it? Is this what your friends ask for? In the case you demand the whole of him it is worth wondering why you have this need. Is it your big ego that makes you expect him to do all your favors, a replacement of your mother or he is someone you feel well being with. Do you expect more things than he is able to give? Do you give more than you are prepared to share? These questions must be answered consciously so as to avoid pain and hurt feelings later.

Let's untangle the knot. Again the choice of a friend should be very conscious. It is of major importance to know why you want to be friends with someone. You have to identify the reasons you regard him or her as your soul mate. The reason of your friendship should be clear on your mind. You must know exactly what you ask from him and what you can offer so that there is action and reaction. If you pinpoint the reasons of your friendship, and be sincere with yourself, things are not complicated.

If you are not fully aware of your choice you are about to feel hurt when this friendship comes to an end. Consider the case that you choose someone just to tell your problems and discuss everything that bothers you. He always listens to you patiently and tries to help you. Every time you need to talk to someone, he is there for you and when you don't feel well, he is willing to meet you. After you express all your feelings you feel better and you consider him your best friend.

Here comes the illusion which has blurred your own emotions and did not let you think clearly. Your friend listens to you, and that's a great feeling of you as you feel secure next to him. But, do you do anything relevant for his needs? If not, the end is on the way. He will start keeping distance from you. The pain is the lesson you must learn. You didn't actually need a friend but a crutch to anchor your sick part of you. You feel lighter from your problems because when a problem is shared it weighs less. Are you able to be in his shoes? It is not easy to carry the burdens of others all the time. His getting tired is a matter of time as nobody endures lifting weight for long. Nobody likes the role of being just a crutch and it is very natural. If you listen to his problems too, it is fine. If you don't, problems are about to start as this friendship is not a two way interaction and balance is nonexistent. This relation is based on insecurity, egoism and hypocrisy. The problem lies to the realization that from the beginning you knew you only needed someone to listen to you. When your friend starts keeping a distance from you and this is absolutely fair and honorable, your hurt feelings come to the surface. You strongly believe that you did not do anything wrong and your friend is just being unfair and took you for granted. Why do feel hurt now? There is probably something you did not understand well, something you misinterpreted. From the moment he refuses to listen to you, you are going to accuse him of betraying your trust, or think that you are the victim of the case.

Can you see how unstable your emotions and beliefs can be? You made it very easy for your battery to run low. All this could have been avoided if every action of yours were well thought and conscious. Your energy levels would have been steady and you would not have suffered all these negative emotions. All it takes is to be cognizant and mindful as far as your actions and beliefs are concerned.

It is exclusively your own decision to stand on your feet without needing someone to make you feel important as long as he may choose to leave you. His choice is absolutely respectable and accepted. Then what? Should you lose the ground under your feet? Do you leave your happiness and energy levels at the mercy of others? Did you learn the lesson? Try to find the lesson you have to learn. Don't choose to remain to pain but see the collateral beauty of your experience. Next time you will be conscious! No reason is so strong as to stop loving yourself.

Always remember that you feel secure only with yourself and no other third party as long as you love and respect yourself, without allowing your big ego to sit in the middle of your mind. Good will is the most important motive to start building a healthy relationship with others. Only then will your burdens feel like a feather. This is because you know exactly what you do, the reason why you choose to act this way and the joy has rung your door bell.

You can see that a non conscious decision may have disastrous results for you. The question is why we choose our self destruction. Why is the idea of being a victim flirting with you and looks attractive? Every true and mutual expression of friendship should be free from egoism which constitutes a hindrance to develop a healthy relation. You must get rid of the fixed idea that you are the only sun that shines. You are the sun in your own universe. Don't forget that others have their own sun too, in their universe and you must respect them. Never forget that everyone is self-illuminated, everyone needs his own space, and everyone has the right to breathe freely, not only you!

The powerful past

Everybody on this planet was born to execute a purpose. A purpose which is necessary to help humanity evolve. Have you ever tried to discover the reason you were born? Have you discussed with your soul? Have you listened carefully to your inner self? If you cannot listen to your soul then try to discover why you have it muted. Nobody else has the power to push you towards a destination if you do not allow him. You are the driver of your own vehicle. If you think that others have more power on you, make the effort to find out why you let it happen. If you are sentimental or shy enough to express your inner voice, then stop complaining. Either you have to learn the lesson or continue going to the opposite direction. But never forget that only you are responsible to direct the flow of your life?

Before you start blaming anyone, start thinking why you allowed it happen. You may say that your parents, the social ethics or the place you grew up are to blame. Ok, that's definitely true. Your parents may not used to leave any room for you to express your voice. It sounds usual but then you were a baby. You were young and you had no power over your wishes.

What happens now? You are an adult, you have a completely formed personality and you can be your own man, the one who has the control of your life. The problem gets bigger when you insist on being stuck to the past. It is definitely not easy to get rid of all the convictions others have imposed on you. Now, you are capable of being your own leader. The only step you have to take is to dare. Dare what? Dare face your soul and find the purpose of your life.

It may also happen because you can't undertake the responsibility in case something goes wrong. It is a safe tactic to protect yourself in case you make a mistake, but you have already made a great misinterpretation. It is time you learnt that mistakes are the lights in the dark to show us the right way. As we have already said, being a victim is the safest way to avoid taking the responsibility in order to avoid pain. But, if *you* can't take the responsibility for yourself, who can? Who do you trust to decode the journey of your soul? I am sure you will say that you want to avoid getting hurt. That's fair! Then do not complain. Stop pretending you are blind and deaf to your wishes.

Being autonomous requires stamina and will power. Then your freedom is before you. Babies trying to learn how to walk are the ideals teachers. They fall down again and again. The amazing lesson is that they stand up with even more enthusiasm to go on. They don't feel losers but they feel great and proud for their every single step. This is the most precious lesson we have to grasp. Even if you feel disappointed, get up and start with another step. Can you imagine where humanity would be if babies stopped trying to walk after their first unfortunate attempt? Walking would be unimaginable.

When you were young, your parents used to take you out in a pushchair. It was their decision to choose the direction. Now you are a grown up, you have your legs and the mind to take any way you like. You do not need them anymore. Now are ready to explore any path your soul desires. Now you don't expect others to feed you. You can decide what you would most like to cook all by yourself. You do not wait others to give you a bath. You can do it on your own. The same way you learnt all these things, you are going to learn to follow your dreams. Love and work are the two magic ingredients to find out your purpose in order to free your soul and help others too.

Loving myself will show me my purpose

There are many fixed beliefs on our minds that cry out for us helping them to put in order. If you still expect your mum or dad to help you, protect you, decide for you, you delay finding your purpose. Finding your purpose means listening to the vibrations of your soul. It means recognizing what makes you really happy, what brightens your heart. Finding your purpose means having your eyes turned inside you, and being faithful to you. You are unique and precious. Don't let yourself get lost in the infinite orbits of others

Try asking people around you, if they have found the purpose of their life, if they managed to be those who they always dreamt of, if they lived the experiences they have always desired, if they have the job they have always dreamt of, you can imagine their answers.

Many will tell you that they had no time, others that they lacked the opportunity, some may blame the structure of society, others will start telling you about their financial or family problems they were unable to overcome. You will see their smile fading when they start talking about their daily routine. Those who prevented them from following their dreams are always the others. They will never admit that they did not work hard enough to achieve their goals. They will never admit that they were afraid to take the responsibility of their happiness.

You definitely know people whose dream was a completely different job from the one they have now. They have chosen the safe way to follow their father's steps, others a job that would make them respectable and a whole lot of people who are just waiting for their retirement. Most of them will tell you various excuses for not doing what their soul cried for.

Another way to avoid the consequences of my actions is to blame my parents or my spouse. A common belief is to accuse them of cutting your wings. They may find thousands of excuses just to feel a victim. Excuses that help you hide your lack of inner power to confess to yourselves that you have not allowed yourselves to find your purpose in life.

In order to find your purpose you need two things. First of all, you need to find yourself. Don't worry, it is somewhere inside you. In order to find yourself, you need to discover you. Accept your strong and weak points and feel grateful for what you are. Being the same with others is not freedom. It is slavery. You follow a path without knowing your destination. You are not purposeful. You are a follower.

Another ingredient for the recipe of finding your purpose is to work towards it. What have you done to free yourself from the tight clothes others have put on you when you were a baby? It is like wearing the same clothes since you were an infant. You definitely feel suppressed without having the initiative of your movements. You buy clothes that you feel comfortable in and when it comes to your soul, you prefer to rely on what makes you feel restricted.

Love yourself! It is not freedom when you choose to be kind with others and hard on yourself. It is not love when you listen to others' problems and get burdened and you ignore your soul telling you that it can't stand this situation any more. It is not wise to respect others and show disrespect to you. It is destructive to talk nicely to others but scold yourself. It is not healthy to hug others but slap yourself. It is not your purpose to love others, but not yourself.

Loving yourself does not mean hating others. When you love yourself you feel inner peace. Your battery has enough energy to give others too. Disorders become when you are out of energy. Then you have no recourses for yourself, let alone others. If you don't have any resources how will you give others? The same applies with money and everything else. If you don't have any, how will you be able to give others?

Even on airplane safety demonstrations, you see that the crew instruct people who accompany children that they must first put on the oxygen mask and then help their children, because if you don't have any, what will you give to others?

It is time we realized that loving me is healthy. Do not confuse it with loving my ego. Loving myself is divine. I am a gift to humanity. I need to remember the purpose I was born for. I need to get rid of all the clothes I used to wear when I was a baby. I need new and bigger ones. Loving myself means knowing myself, accepting myself, appreciating myself and respecting my purpose on this planet. Loving me is feeling the connection with the star dust. Loving me is discovering all the glitter and all the light that is inside me.

See the difference between the people who have lived their life as the wanted and the people who did nothing to find their purpose in life. Instead, they followed the purpose others wanted for them. Those who have achieved their goals and followed their purpose their soul asked for are full of energy. Actually, they have managed to maintain and collect more energy than the amount they were born with. These people are not afraid of death, either. They know that the energy they have now is at higher levels and they have come closer to the Big Light, God. Those who haven't managed to collect and save their resources, they lack energy. They have less energy than their initial resources. They did not respect the gift they were given by their birth. These people are afraid of death because instead of getting closer to the Light of Life they have gone the other way, and the distance is longer.

How can I find the purpose of my life?

In order to recall the purpose I came to achieve in this life, we have to discover who we really are, and work towards this direction. You may start thinking about the moments you feel happy, what makes you feel satisfied, when you feel proud of yourself, when you congratulate yourself. A good technique is writing down the times you really appreciated your efforts, your successes, the times you felt that mission was accomplished.

Remember all the course of action you followed that led you to these happy moments. The reason you wanted to do it. What the motives were and the possible hardships you had to overcome. When you pinpoint all the necessary emotions, feelings and actions taken, you have made the first step. All long distances start with a first step. No great feat was easy.

A helping hand would be to realize that your life is your choice in order to evolve. You chose to be the first or second or third child, you chose these parents, and you chose your whole course here. And this is very important because it will help us remember what we have to achieve. All aspects of our lives are carefully designed by us before we were born. Now, it needs work to remember what lesson I need to take in order to advance to a higher class. All the lessons that will help me lead me to a higher grade are here, waiting for me. Neither school children understand why they go to school at first. It takes years, even a whole life to appreciate the fruits of their hard work.

It is exactly the same with us now. All problems lead to a solution. It's no use complaining over it, but solving it will take us further, to a new chapter. Whether you understand it or not, has little importance to humanity. Try to enjoy it and do it with pleasure because the results are unavoidable. Your conscious choice lies to whether you get all the satisfaction of it or all the pain.

If you reach the point of discovering your inner purpose, you will be able to appreciate all the things you have managed, everything you have offered and feel proud of. You will recognize when these love feelings were greater. Try to feel the advanced levels of your battery at those moments you felt happy, balanced, optimistic and full of love. The resources of love were enough to share with others too. That's a great step to move on.

Secondly, you have to discover your interests. Try to pinpoint why football, or painting, or reading makes you get away from it all. Notice the wall paper of your personal computer. Why did you choose it? When do you feel well during the day? What causes you distress feelings? Why? The key factor here is not to blame others. If you can't, try to find out why someone beyond you, has the power to influence your mood. Which door did you leave open and he managed to enter?

The key factor is to know when you feel contented. You have the power to adopt this behavior and consciously avoid situations that lower your energy levels. The choice is only yours. If that hurts others, it is their problem to close their door. Not yours. You live in you. Everybody lives in a separate house. Everybody is responsible to keep their house safe from intruders.

Self confirmation is self realization. When we know who we are, our real purpose comes out on the surface, we adopt the behavior of our good self, we fill the gaps and we get accustomed to being kind and protective towards our soul.

How can I define my goals?

Look again at the experiences you have written down. Watch every aspect of yourself, recognize what your real interests are, the books you read, people that move you, situations that touch your inner cord, moments that affect you. This way, you have most of the pieces of the puzzle. Now start working on what touches the inner cords of you. When do you feel happy? Why do you feel betrayed? What can you do to avoid stressful situations? It is high time you recognized your true self. You are a whole and complete universe. Follow your orbit. You have the power to feed yourself with all the love energy which is infinite out there. Don't choose to be a deformed personality. You do not deserve it. You were not born to be friends with pain.

Don't feel guilty when your goals change. This is absolutely natural. Our goals change according to our experiences, our realizations, our age, our advancement. It is like changing the wallpaper on your computer or your signature. The purpose of people 500 years ago was totally different from now. This is evolution. This is the flow of universe. Don't try to resist going according to the flow of your soul. If you decide to go the other way, think about the pain it may cause, the struggle you are going to experience and how further away you distance from your purpose. Not realizing that you have taken the wrong way on time, it will cost you time, energy and negative feelings of failure.

Now, get down to work. Be aware of the levels of your resources, your interests, your abilities, and your inner power. I can't be a teacher if I don't love kids. I can't be a gymnast if I hate exercising. I can't be a professor if I am not interested in studying. I can't be a right parent if I am not ready to be devoted to those I love. I can't be a good listener if my inner need is to talk only about my problems. I can't be a doctor if I don't like helping others. As you can see, self realization is the secret key of your hidden door.

In other words, we must have the power to organize our life towards the achievement of our purpose. Here is a trap. Many times we are influenced, we admire or wish to look like people due to their financial state or their personality without knowing anything about their daily burdens, skills, struggles, pressures or abilities. We look at the surface of their lives, not being aware of the sacrifices they make. The internal side of things hides real truth. A complete aspect of our goal is necessary to be acquired in order to make it clear if we want to work towards this goal out of pleasure or hands out are your motive to head towards this goal. A good idea is to spend some trial time next to a professional doing the job you want to follow. This way we have the opportunity to see if it really suits us, not just by being attracted by his earnings. Only by acquiring a spherical view of it, will we be able to recognize if this is our real dream.

The role of parents

Parents are the first to help us when we are at a young age. They are our heroes. They teach us everything. If they knew how to move their ears, we would also know how to do it. They are those who understand our physical needs when we are babies. They know when we are hungry, thirsty, when we need a hug. To our eyes they are gods. We see them walking when we can't, listen to them talking while we can't and they are those we rely on to help us develop our faith. Children know that when they cry, a bottle of milk or open hands are waiting for them. All these feelings of safety, admiration, love can't be easily deleted by our hidden memory. It's a mystery how easily we forget being faithful to us now, as we are responsible for our well-being.

Parents are those who teach us how to write and read, what is right or wrong, and they even tell us how to act and react. They take us where they believe we will have a nice time. In a pushchair! Remember? That's correct up to a point. When we grow up we are able to walk towards the way our soul pushes us. The problem is when parents can't accept that we have formed our own personality and it is time we decided ourselves which way to follow. It is really difficult to cut the invisible umbilical cord which unites them with their kids. They definitely have more experience about life and they want to protect and keep us safe. Safe from what? Our real dreams? Our divine flow? It is this misunderstood fixed feeling that it is only them who can do it and forget the role of our Great

Father and Mother. They forget that we have our own star dust. They forget that we are conducts of our energy flows.

It often happens to wrongly believe that their dreams are automatically their kids' dream. They may insist on their kids following their job out of the belief that their experience may save them time, money and failure. According to their belief, guiding their kids to follow the field they have been successful will automatically make their kids successful too. Another way they trust they help them is to direct them towards the field they haven't managed to enter due to various reasons. Their unfulfilled dreams become the purpose of their kids. It may be so, but there are many other parameters to think of.

First of all, they never take seriously the possibility how this kind of love, because they do it out of love and nobody can deny that, may cause mental and physical health problems to their children. They don't do it on purpose of course. This is what, in turn, they were taught when they were kids. It is their firm belief that they know better. This firm belief of theirs may be their big firm ego hidden behind the name of love. They just forget that having the experience of life doesn't automatically means knowing the purpose of their kids' life. Of course, parents' main aim is to do their best for their kids, they love their children more than their own life, and they can die unconditionally in order to save their kids. These facts bear no doubt. But they have to realize the mechanism which is under this belief. Their fulfilled or unfulfilled dream does not unquestionably mean it is their kids' dream as well. They forget that there may be a possibility that their kids were born to serve another purpose in the evolution of humanity.

All parents want genius kids, with unique personalities that lead them to self realization. Everyone is proud of children who stand on their own feet, work hard and succeed in what they do. How can I stand on my own feet, when my mum always told me what to do? How can I discover my talents when she always tried to help me avoid pain? Some parents want clever students and they think this is achieved by doing every exercise correctly. Sometimes they even solve mathematics problems for them. Is it the grade that matters more than finding out the way to think right? How can they be tomorrow winners if they are not taught how to fight? What I mean is that they have food ready on their kids' plate and sometimes they even chew the food for them. How will kids learn this way to identify their favorite flavor?

They believe it is a defect, a flaw or blemish if their kids can't learn something as quickly as they want, or the way they think it the right one. So they try to hide it from others and even from their kid too. They may blame the teacher and support their kid just to make him feel superior. Have they ever thought that this tactic will lead their kid having a false idea about himself? What about the shock he is going to suffer when he gets out of his nest and enters the real face of society? What about his hurt feelings when he realizes that he is not the one his parents used to lead him believe he is? That he is not the smartest one or the most beautiful or the best?

In this case, without being conscious of the results, parents harm their kids and they will also be hurt when they realize it. Think of the case where a mother always puts the right books for school in her child's school bag, checks everything is its place and he has not forgotten anything at home. Or the case where the mother or father carries the schoolbag for their kids. They believe they are helpful and they serve their purpose perfectly. Another misunderstood feeling is on our way.

They teach their kids that they always need someone to support them, as they are not able to do for themselves what they were supposed to, according to their age. Have they ever wandered what is the message they pass on to their kids? That they are unable to do what other kids at their age find easy and natural. Parents pass to their kids' subconscious the fact they are useless, they can manage nothing without others' help. And believe me, when such beliefs become second nature to them, they won't even try to achieve anything. They are going to spend their whole lives at the shade of others and feel hurt every time others' help is denied.

The belief that they can have everything from those who love them will follow them for the rest of their life. They are going to seek their parents back up in their friends or partners. Who is willing to play the role of the other's mother? This will lead to the breakup of the relation and the kid will never understand what went wrong. Then, he may start believing that he can't find real love or real friendships do not exist.

Here the lesson we have to learn is to think deeper and take on our responsibilities. Nobody is inferior to us, there are people smarter than us, there are people more beautiful than us, but we are unique. False beliefs are those who hurt us. Not us. We deserve the best as long as we do what corresponds to us and take on our responsibilities. Just stop thinking that everyone is as enthusiastic as our mum to bring us our slippers and put them on our feet. It needs work. And this work should be done by us. Go get them. When we do more things about us, then we will realize that we are able to stand on our feet and need nobody to serve us. This is independence. And independence means freedom. The real feeling of freedom and appreciation are the starting point to love ourselves. To be more precise, either you realize and change it, or think forever that nobody loves you like your mum and get hurt. You choose!

It is food for thought to realize that those who love me more than their own life, deprive me of the chance of reaching self realization. Isn't that a great utopia? However, if parents do not be as helpful as they believe they should be, they may feel guilty of not raising their kids in the right way. Kids may also accuse them of not helping them enough. But this is their problem. This is not the case. Everyone must feel happy, complete and satisfied. Let's see what the laws of nature have to teach us.

Nature is undoubtedly our greatest teacher. Every plant knows exactly when to blossom, without having a calendar or a watch. Plants try to give you the best of their fruit, because they know that if their fruit is sour, it is a matter of time to become extinct. Think of a tree that gave bitter fruits. After some time nobody would plant it as nobody would like to eat it. It will disappear and nobody would feel sorry about it. But when a tree offers you sweet fruits, you protect it and you take care of it, and you even try to multiply it. What does it teach us? This teaches us that if we give our best of us, others will appreciate it and love us. If we behave in a bitter way, we will stand out there alone and hurt.

Another reason they offer you their fruit is to save their "children". Let's see how it works. When you pick fruit, you plant the core away from the "mother" tree at a place that it is sunny, and free from weed. This is the only way a plant can grow naturally and grow healthy. By being able to breathe freely and having access to the sun. Trees take advantage of you in order to ensure their continuation. They know that the more and better fruit they give, the more their species are going to survive. They are not mean or stingy. The natural law is action and reaction. They could have more easily thrown their seed just under their branches, but nature knows that no plant is well grown under the shade of the big tree. It needs room and light to spread their branches. So do kids. They need room to unfold and spread their thoughts, experiences and actions and light in order to absorb it and let it sparkle in their soul.

I am going to give you another example to make it more explicit. Suppose each one of us came to this world in order to learn and play a musical instrument and claim a seat in the great orchestra of humanity. If my destiny instrument is the piano, I spend many years to learn how to play it, I spend many years rehearsing, correcting, changing so that when time comes, I am ready to deserve a place in the great orchestra of humanity, I must be very well prepared and well tuned. All my experiences, the hardships I have been through, the good and difficult moments of my life, teach me how to play and preserve my piano better.

If my kid's instrument is the guitar, and I am convinced I can help him tune his guitar, the way I tune my piano due to my experiences the result would be an awful discordance. Do I want my kid to be a cacophony? Of course this is not my purpose as a parent. On the other hand I have difficulty in accepting the fact that I don't know! I was taught that parents know everything. Hello, big ego again! And what happens in case my kid has to learn the tzouras and I don't even know what a tzouras is? How tragic would the results be? The absolute discordance was created by my invisible ego. And it is me, the one who loves him more who caused this pain. Is there a chance of his getting a seat in the great orchestra? No, he does not deserve it. He has not gone through the necessary procedures to learn, he has made no rehearsals, and he has not worked because I did not let him room to rehearse. He only cheated, but unfortunately he copied the wrong answers. The answers *I* gave him, because I thought I was smarter than him. He lost his place and my love has been transformed to his absolute failure. A loss for his chance to get to know himself, a chance to get accustomed with himself, a chance to feel full and happy, a chance to love himself.

Everything happened on the name of love. The defeat is the result on the name of his happiness. But the consequences are detrimental and he is going to carry them on his back for the rest of his life. Out of the purest of motives! A wrongly interpreted love made him miserable. Now I may start praying to get rid of everything I have taught him.

Many times when there is an argument between parents and children, the hidden message this shouting conveys is: "Mum, if you love me, don't love me" meaning if you love me, behave as if you don't love me. Raise me as you didn't care and leave me alone to discover the path my soul has left on the snow. They are there to show me the way" It is difficult for parents to say goodbye to the big ego, as separations are painful, but this one is lifesaving. It is going to free their kids for the rest of their lives.

Parents need and ought to be next to their kids and not on their heads. Listening to their wishes and needs carefully will be of great help. Egoism has no room in this relationship. The belief that my experiences make me a genius life translator is totally wrong. Experiences are endless and every person has his own different ones. How self centered do I become when I believe I know everything? I have to accept that there is no problem if my kids' wishes are different from mine. There is no problem if I can't understand theirs as long as they feel happy and secure. The purpose is not to block their way. My purpose is to let them evolve and grow naturally, and I am there to remind them that I am next to them when they need me. Only when they need my help and not intrude in their wishes.

Every brain, every soul is unique. I have no power and right to direct anyone. How will evolution come if I we are stuck to old beliefs, morals and ethics. Every new experience tries to tell us something. Let's embrace it and stop fearing of going out of our comfort zone. Let's welcome and approve of every new knowledge and experiences and forget the past. Let's open the windows of our mind to let the new light of sun come in. Every day new beams reach us. It is no use looking for the past ones.

Many times kids feel happier when parents express a special weakness to a kid. They feel charmed and enjoy this feeling. Sometimes, they perceive it as greater love. Let's see what the word says. Weak! Has it ever crossed your mind that they regard him as weak and have power over him? This could mean that he is not strong enough to stand up for his rights. It is obvious that a child with a strong personality and determination to do what pleases him and not his parents is not always the one that attracts parents' sensitivity. Usually mothers are attached to more vulnerable kids as they have more chances to influence them. And the irony is that some parents feel so fulfilled when their kids cannot say not to them. They think they have succeeded their target. No, the target of a parent is to responsibly raise their kids and accept their different universe.

Our mental functions

Another very important factor which must not be disregarded is that of what makes us unique. Every person is moved by a different mental function. Others are moved by sentiments, others by thinking, others by senses, and others by intuition. Some people like material things, others feel complete when they use their fantasy and create a painting or a song, some leave their decisions to their intuition and others judge according to their sentimental state. Some feel secure when they belong to a high social class while others when their self is their best friend. Some people use first their rational thoughts before acting, others trust their feeling, others get great pleasure out of smelling, touching or constructing things. Some people rely on their intuition to make up their mind. Everyone has these functions but what differentiates us is the percentage we have them. We need to be open and respect everyone's unique function. Nothing is wrong or right. It is a terrible mistake and egoistic to think that whatever does not suit me is wrong.

The point is not trying to change others, but accepting others. As we have said before, everyone is born with different talents, different purposes and different functions. I can't judge others according to my limited ability to accept anything different from my fixed ideas. This is not the natural law of flow. The healthy part is to find out why I can't accept that other people are moved by different impulses and react in a different way. What keeps me tied is that I can't understand how other functions work. When

I understand how this mechanism works and contributes to our personality, it is easy to understand others. This realization will help me avoid painful feelings that deprive me of my inner balance and health.

Suppose a boy's first function is thought and his second is sensation. A job that would suit him would be one that could satisfy these two main functions. He could be a great doctor, an efficient mechanic, a chemist, whatever needs these stronger functions of his character, thinking and sensing. Suppose his father is the owner of a successful accounting office with a great number of clients. His ego does not let him see that the dream he chose to fulfill does not suit his son. He feels that it is a shame to close down his business when he retires. He has invested money, time and a lot of hard work. His ego does not let him see that what freed him may imprison his son. He would never understand that his son would be happier if he became a painter or a director. We will probably try to persuade his son to study finance and accounting in order to be the successor of his business.

If his son follows the wish of his father, he may be in a safe job but his soul has nowhere to lean. Numbers cannot be touched, and his soul asks for it. He could not say no to his father and he chose to say no to his mental functions that show him the way to express his innate talents. The outcomes here depend on how strong the willpower of his son is. If he does what his dad wants, sooner or later, he may start having some psychosomatic problems as his first functions are not fulfilled. If he is prepared to follow what his inner voice tells him, he is going to close down the accounting office and do what he wants.

In this case, social rumors also play an important role which determines our mood and mental health. People may start criticizing him that the son proved unable to continue a profitable office. We have to realize again that this is their problem. We must not be affected by what others say. Nobody knows you as well as you.

Moreover, the father may feel so depressed and disappointed that his son did not appreciate a whole life's struggles. Not to mention that he will try to prove that all he had done was for his son. He would never mention that he followed his dream and he ought to let his son free to follow his. If this decision was taken consciously, then, nobody is going to influence the son's happiness levels. Nobody else has the ability to change the way your soul shows you to proceed. Only your soul knows your real purpose of life.

Our mental functions are very important to be discovered because they can reveal much valuable information about our personality and talents. They are like a light in the desert waiting for someone to cross this distant place and be seen. You are the one who has instant access to this part of yours. Of course an analytical graphological analysis from a specialist could help you discover them.

All these examples are used to explain that in every aspect of our life we see that real security can't survive if we don't follow our hearts and our intuition. Our inner voice must find open ears to be heard. Only this way can it help us discover our talents. Otherwise, we are delayed and so is humanity. Evolution knows no restrictions and it pushes us to go on. It is our misunderstanding fixed ideas that we grasp as pain.

The golden and most precious rule is to be faithful to yourself. Don't behave to you the way you would never behave to others. Listen and respect yourself. To put it simple, love yourself.

Always have in mind that our goals are relevant to our purpose and are based on important values. The way we act should be the way that leads us to our fulfillment. Our purposes are not one way. It is multi dimensional. We can be good citizens, good parents, good workers, good friends, good scientists, good husbands, and so on. Being well is a conscious decision that leaves no room to unwelcome intruders.

Changing the misinterpreted beliefs

Some people are considered to be shy. What does this mean? Was he born shy? They are usually people who choose for their own security and due to their own insecurity to hide behind their parents, their friends, their husband or wife. I am sure you know a lot of people who would avoid talking on the phone even to order a pizza. The people around them take it for granted and accept their shyness. Do others really help them this way? Can you live a whole life hiding from what makes you feel uncomfortable?

The most paradox belief is that we want to change the result, but not the course of action. Is that possible? Of course not. The result will change only by changing our actions. How else can reaction happen? If an incident arises and this shy person is forced to be the leader, he will feel uncomfortable and insecure just because this is the first time he is forced to change. Let the battle begin.

The only way to learn is by pain. Fear is the avoidance of pain. There is no other way to learn. Can you number the things you could do if your shyness disappeared in a magic way? Now think of the times you wanted to react but suppressed your feelings. Do you believe that your cells enjoy this suppression? Definitely not! How can they tell you that they suffer? Is there any other way for them to tell you that you don't respect them than an illness? I don't think so! The choice is yours! Respect your cells or wait to see the results of their revolution. Don't feel comfortable in your emotional weakness. Sometimes change is freedom.

When you have discovered what keeps you back, it is time you started loving yourself. Make a little step at a time. Think why all the "musts" are included in your daily vocabulary? Why must your house be tidy all the time? What will happen if some time you don't feel like cleaning up? What will happen if your child wants to help you do the cake together and breaks a plate? It won't take you more than five minutes to clean it up, but a raised voice and punishment won't be forgotten for a long time.

You "must" always be helpful, in good spirits, cook in time, sleep in time, wash the dishes in time, and visit your aunt every Sunday. How can you transform this "must" into "want"? It is easier said than done but it is worth the trial. Only by charging your battery will you achieve this transformation. If you feel that you choke in your every day routine, stop and think! How do you charge your battery? I mean, what you do in order to relax and get away from it all. Notice that you "must" cook for the family when you are tired and pressed for time, but you "want" to please them with a nice meal after an outing to the movies with your friends.

It is worth trying to find a hobby or a pastime that allows you to get you out of the house. Who decided that you are able to do all the things you do? Who chose the way you live? Whose idea was that you reached the point of feeling like a machine? Certainly yours, probably because this was the way you grew up, or the way you always thought was the right one. Right for whom? Here comes the difficult question. What do you do to change all that? Don't start telling that things can't change. Don't say that it is too late to change. No, that's a defeat. Your "musts" have beaten your "wants". All this is just excuses. What will happen if one day you are unable to mop the floor, or cook? Will the earth stop revolving? Of course not. Will you throw someone out of his comfort? That's his problem. Everyone deserves to act the way they feel and pleases himself too and not just others.

A worthwhile activity to please yourself won't take more than two to four hours a week. It's not a big deal. How come you have time for everything else and not for yourself? I hope you realize that this is not logical. Doing an activity such as jogging, cycling, painting, dancing, going to the movies, joining a club, doing something constructive, funny, pleasing is so simple and so revitalizing at the same time. It just takes the courage to change and give it a try. But don't judge the result before you even try.

If you don't want to change your stressful routine, then stop nagging. You are worthy of your fate. If you fancy living with the real meaning of the word, then move. Change your habits. Open your heart and stop choosing pain instead of healing. I am going to tell it again and again. You were born to be happy and not suffer. Only you are responsible for your emotional state. You have to find which gap you left open and start working towards fixing it.

Another confrontation with your inner peace takes place when you don't reveal your true feelings and you hesitate telling "No". Maybe you are afraid and it is fine, as long as you know what you are afraid of. Is it your fear of taking the responsibility of losing a friend who does not respect your wishes? Do you hesitate to dissatisfy someone who only thinks how to achieve his purpose no matter what? You used to say yes to your parents when you were five and you didn't know any other way to stand on your feet. Now, you are twenty five, or thirty five or fifty five and you know. You know what makes you happy and what causes you misery. You know what you want and what you dislike. Why can't you respect your true feelings? Nobody is going to scold you now. You have nobody to be afraid of. Don't let negative feelings from the past govern your present. You only have to love yourself. Love and respect your inner being.

Recognizing the problem is redemption. The fact that you feel uncomfortable is the way to learn to feel comfortable every single moment. The moment we feel that everything goes wrong is the moment your redemption reveals. Calm down, take deep breaths and listen to your soul's voice. Feel safe! It leads you out of the dungeon you used to hide your true self. Yes, a happy life is out there and it is waiting for you. You only have to climb to the top and get out. The light will show you the right way. Just follow it.

Fixed roles

It is a common belief in many societies that people must act according to some principles. Boys, for instance, must know how to play football and the right toy for girls are dolls and they ought to be themselves as pretty as dolls. Who set these stereotypes and what is the purpose they serve? Society? Media? Ethics? What if a boy hates football and a girl is not as pretty as others expect? Is this trait of them that defines how smart, kind, grateful they are? Who told you that not being in perfect shape brings misery and automatically makes you unaccepted? Why is it acceptable for a businessman to have an affair with a much younger lady, but an older woman having an affair with a younger man is considered improper in many societies?

Why is crying considered a womanish habit? Why is it considered as a weakness for men? Many times, when boys start crying, dads say that men don't cry! Let's analyze it a bit further. Let's turn to the internal function of the eye. When do eyes produce tears? When something has entered your eye and it needs to be thrown away. Purification is the cause that eyes produce tears. Combine the facts. When you feel like crying is catharsis. Something beyond you, touched you, entered your soul due to your connection with it and triggered your need for sentimental catharsis. Why is there the fixed belief that men's soul does not need catharsis?

Is it healthy to tell someone to stop crying? This way we prevent the catharsis of his soul. We force him to swallow all the negative feelings, instead of getting rid of them. I don't think that we have the right to tell someone to keep dirt in his soul just because others say that this is against the expected principles. The only thing I manage to do is to delay him because when he is left alone he is going to cry. Of course he will not solve his problem but this is the procedure to understand that there is no point in worrying over spilt milk. This is his chance to see what forced him to cry. There is definitely something that he did not understand well, or his ego has sneaked in again.

A common phrase to console someone is telling him "I understand you". How can I understand him? Have I been through the same situation? Do we have the same mental functions? In essence, I tell lies to him and delay him again to solve his problem.

Turning problems into opportunities

When a friend of ours does not feel well or he goes through a difficulty, we use to tell him to go out in order to forget his problem. We even insist on it as it is our firm belief that this will make him feel better or find solution to what occupies his mind. We believe that we do the right thing to help him forget his worries. What we haven't realized is that the point is not to forget the problem but solve it. And the only way to solve it is to realize it. To find the internal source of all these distressed feelings.

Another false belief that prevents us from being balanced is the fact that we do not realize that some feelings are not our true expression, but is accepted socially. It is important to become strong enough and understand that our real feelings are what matters and not what others have taught us to believe. We are used to adopting other peoples' beliefs. For example, if someone loses his job he is automatically overwhelmed with negative feelings and pessimism. It is a firmed belief that everyone who loses his job should feel worried.

Negativism is stronger than optimism. Most people would tell me that I have lost my mind if I feel happy when I lose my job. The point is to remain apathetic and look on the bright side of life. We must trust our Creator. We must trust our flow. Closing a door, gives you the chance to open another one. We are not able to see the case that the door that opens may bring us before a better job and that's why we feel insecure. There is no other way to know the result until we try. What we lack is trust. This prevents us from facing the loss of a job as a chance for a better one. This causes us neglect our own entity and try to live through the eyes of others. We have adopted a strong belief that prevents us from going on. Regardless it is a common belief or not, we have to solve it ourselves. We must trust that our birth is not accidental. We are a product of love, and love is all around us. It is a pity to let others keep my eyes closed. Open them and look in front of you. Faith and work is all you need to go further than others imagined you could get.

The same happens with affairs. The expected social beliefs make those who are single feel quite excluded. They feel that something is wrong with them and others find nothing to love in them. There are deeper reasons this is happening. First of all, I am the only one who must love me. Not out of egoism, but in order to feel secure with myself and my choices. Only then will I not be influenced by social beliefs. If I don't love myself and I don't feel comfortable with my soul, it will lead me to believe that my partner is my savior and I must do everything that pleases him. This "must" is not healthy. A love affair should not be based on obligation or fear of loneliness.

Love involves a higher connection. It has nothing to do with social norms. We have told it many times, and I am going to tell it many more. Every decision you make should be with complete conscience. Suppose I have a problem finding the right partner even though others find me quite pretty. Here applies the misunderstood notion that only the pretty ones deserve a handsome boyfriend. Who has passed this on you? Remember? Definitely, not you. But it is true that when a girl is pretty it is difficult for others to imagine that she does not have a boyfriend. If this lasts for long, we start wondering if there is something wrong with her personality or manners. Is that love? Do you think that real love is based on appearance? Do I communicate with the outer part of a person? It is all wrong!

Personality includes our physical, our sentimental and our notion. If people choose to love someone according to what they see, fate will force them to look deeper and it is a matter of time to look deeper. It is painful, but this is the procedure to have a spherical aspect of everything.

Let's analyze the case I don't have a boyfriend for a long time when all my friends do. This may bring bitter feelings to someone who is not able to see the reason it is happening. Actually, this means you are not able to see the internal message universe sends you. You are not ready to advance to a higher grade. They stick to negativism and choose to embrace pain. In such a case, it will just take you longer to learn, whether you like it or not. If this is what I feel, there are two ways to get over it. One way out, is to substitute the situation. That is to face it. I start wondering if a new haircut would made me look more attractive, if I stopped criticizing others, or talking with more respect to others would make me more approachable. It crosses my mind that socializing by joining a dancing or a painting club would also help. I have pinpointed the problem, found my weak part and start working towards the solution. That is advancement because if I am arrogant and think that nobody is better than me, it means that I see myself through the eyes of my mum, where I was her only princess. Of course, this kind of change is actually realization of misunderstood notions and it leads us a step forward. Full conscience is required so that I take off the clothes others have put on me when I was a baby.

On the other hand, you subconsciously choose to cover the problem. That is to abandon the problem, to place the problem somewhere outside you and get rid of your responsibility. Then, in order to excuse yourself from the responsibility you may say that "all men are pigs". We all know that something like that is impossible to be true, but it makes you feel better because you have no responsibility. It is a common fact that we will always be vulnerable and subconsciously hate whoever tells us the truth. We may feel that nobody loves us, relations and society has changed and the world has become a worse place with arrogant and mean people with real men being scarce.

It is the easiest way to react if I want to avoid facing the light by working. However, if I think deeper I can realize my mistake, but I feel more comfortable if this realization never comes to me. I feel safer, and I do not have the need to get out of my comfort zone. It is like a child refusing to go to high school because he feels safer remaining at the primary school. Will you let him there? Of course not. We have to realize that working with ourselves will take us further. Otherwise, the result will be to stand on an unstable stability and leave it to fate which way it will choose to take you. It is like being on an ungoverned boat. What you have to realize is that the choice is yours to govern your life.

All this happens because you don't understand the deficiency that is natural to our planet. Or you will solve the problem yourself or else you will always need someone to pamper you. This happens because your mum used to cover the problem. She used to say that you are the prettiest, the cleverest, the best. And when you come out to real life, you realize that there are prettier, cleverer and better people than you. Then you feel the slapping on your face. You put the blame on others, but this is not the way to overcome the problem and make use of all the strengths you have.

Realization saves souls. Is it likely to be likeable to everyone? How possible is it to do everything right? Won't you ever fail? Won't you ever feel betrayed, or upset? Why do you still try to lean on somebody expecting him to tell you that it is not your fault? Take on your responsibilities and start working so that you turn into a bright star. Nobody bothers with stars that are not bright and visible. Your brightness comes from your core, your soul. Free yourself and bright up. You owe it to yourself and to humanity. Your light will help others see clearly too.

Being resilient and understand that everyone is different and has his own talents and his own weaknesses is improvement. Anger and misery is the way that leads you to the solution. How else will you learn? If your mum always told you that it is not your fault but your teacher's mean character that your grade was lower than what you had expected, what did she do? Did she protect you? At that time you felt protected and you loved your mum, but in essence, she didn't help you realize your true strengths and weaknesses. She covered you in order to protect you. However, instead of helping you, she enclosed you in a pink bubble. Can you imagine it? It is a matter of time to suffocate. And who did it to you? The one who loved you more than her own life. It is again these unconscious beliefs. It is not that your mum did it on purpose. That's because, that was what she was taught, and she did not know any other way. She lived her own suffocation too. Let's forget the pain and stick to the fact that her mistakes show you the way to get further on, to evolve and advance. We grew up with the belief that loving you means protecting you. You did not know then, but you know now. Stand on your own feet and go on.

You know that if you keep relying on those false beliefs, when you are left alone and someone else tells you the truth, your problem will start becoming evident. It is important to realize that every problem starts when you think of it. It hadn't been there before you placed it, nor everybody else has it. So, problems have to do with the way you wind you brain. Discover the root but enjoy the fruits. The root is there to do its job. What you have to do is take pleasure out of the great a valuable person you are.

We have the tendency to cover problems, to hide them deeply inside us because we expect others to tell us that it is ok and I shouldn't have worried. And do you know why? Just to avoid work! No, that's over coverage and when the truth is revealed it comes as a shock to us. Our whole universe collapses or better we think it collapses. Actually, it collapses just because it is time we looked ahead without having anything to block your vision.

So, every time you feel upset or down in the dumps, stop and think. Who is responsible for feeling this way? Only you! It is time you learned to close your doors to any pollutant of your soul. We are here to enjoy life, and realize that every problem has something to tell us. It is here to teach us not to worry, because real protection comes from greater powers, much higher than we can imagine.

Most of our problems stem from the past and all our anxieties concern our future. We miss every moment of now because we remember old problems or because we place obstacles in front of us. How sad it is to live with painful memories or worries about tomorrow? What about now? Do I dig a muddy puddle to fall into, with my own hands? Why do I choose to do fall into the trap than pass over it? Try to remember who taught you this tactic. Whoever did it, was a victim himself, he is not to blame. He deserves our sympathy because he didn't know, but we do, and this is our power.

Our passing from this world is to collect experiences to enrich our mind library. If I have never eaten beans before, how can I describe them to you? So, I have to try them in order to know. Take school for example. I know the curriculum of the third year, I feel safe there and I don't want to move on to the forth. I know the teacher, the lessons, and I am encircled in my comfort zone. I chose to avoid feeling uncomfortable. Can I move on if I do not want anything to rock my boat? And if I remain in the same year at school, will I acquire everything school provides me with? Of course not. Why then choose to remain in the same position and same aspect of life? As we have said, everything that causes pain has its roots to the past and our refusal to work.

Change is a step forward. If your children told you that they want to repeat the same year at school for another five years because they feel great there, would you allow them? I don't think so. You would definitely start telling him about the new things they are going to learn and the more they know, the happier they will be, the better understanding about the world they are going to acquire. Why do you choose to remain at the same spot for yourself and are afraid to move forwards?

The key point is to learn the lesson and forget the pain. Every time you are hurt, think about the gap you left open, realize why it caused pain to you and get rid of it before it is stuck on your mind. The more it stays there, the harder you will get rid of it. Try to delete it, before it becomes a permanent habit.

Try to change your thoughts, and avoid talking about it as fatalism. The vibrations of your words will bring it back. There is always the collateral beauty of something bad. It may reveal itself later, but our ego does not allow us to be patient. We want it to happen "now". It's our mere ego that causes that. What it needs is to advance our consciousness and learn the lesson with no struggle and pain. For these reasons:

- Don't be afraid to get out of your comfort zone
- Pinpoint exactly what you want, how you choose to live your life and not how others expect you do so.
- Don't judge the way you feel. We usually characterize our sentiments as bad or good, according to previous experiences we had. Bad and good are just definitions to show the way you are polarized.
- Don't forget that every moment is a new "now" and we ought to live it to the full.
- Don't take important decisions when you are very angry or upset nor in full happiness. Try to see the situation from high above, with neutral eyes.
- Don't accept a problem created by others to affect your emotional state to such an extent that you lose your inner balance and your control.

Think that every problem has a goal to score. Surpass the problem and focus on what you need to change or improve so as to tear the nets.

Believing in myself prevents pain

When I ask others whether they like my new haircut or T-shirt, it means that I don't believe in my taste. If they tell me it suits me perfect even though they think it is awful, out of just being kind, they don't protect me. They do it because they don't want to upset me. That is not a normal reaction. If I don't learn the truth, I will be in a delicate bubble; ready to burst. Then, comes the time I am exposed to the truth. At this point I have to wonder why they told me lies. Is it the fact that I do not tolerate anything else but good words? This lies to my false belief that I am perfect and I make no mistakes. Hello big ego! Do I lose my temper when a different opinion is told as mine should be the only correct one? Sit down big ego! I forget the most important part. I asked them. I was not sure if this haircut suits me. I did not believe in my decision. I do not feel safe with myself! Why do I keep blaming others then? I was the one who gave them this power over me.

If others tell me something bad, that may even insult me, I have to look for the reason they told this to me. If I feel insulted, it means I believe it. Suppose you told a basketball player that he is short. His only reaction would be to laugh. If they tell me that I am short, and I believe it, I will surely feel insulted. Why? Because someone else, someone beyond me, made me believe it. I was not born with this belief. I was born to love and respect every part of me. I was born to enjoy every single moment I live.

If I am asked about my opinion about someone's T-shirt and my truth is that it does not suit him, I ask the other person if he wants to do boxing. If he says not, I just don't express my opinion and change subject. If I hide the truth on purpose, I expose the other one to a false reality, which may hurt him when he realizes it. Let's be honest, without the slightest need to deceive others. Let's learn to appreciate true attitudes, even though they get me out of my comfort zone. If others do not stand my sincere truth then I help them advance too.

If I believe in myself, no comment can touch me and affect my mood. The question is asked only when I have doubts. Nobody really cares about my haircut or my T-shirt, nor if my nose is beautiful. My nose is nice if it breaths, not if it straight, or turned up.

If someone loves me, he must fall in love with me as a whole, or I don't want him. If he loves only my face, my beautiful eyes or my delicate body, it means that is only attracted by one trait of mine and he may believe he can change the rest of me. Real love is the whole packet of me, my body and personality as part and parcel. No makeup can fool others for long. Let's not choose to hide our real face. Then, it is a matter of time for truth to be revealed. Procrastinating the truth does not mean it disappears. We just fool ourselves. Many times we don't tell what bothers us because we, ourselves choose to feel stressed. Nobody says theories when he acts. Nobody cares about what you know, what you think of, what you read about. What it really matters is what you do. Your actions become the lesson you teach. Respecting others means giving them, if you feel like it of course, what they need and not what you think they need. Here comes the strength of our soul. Will you help someone the way you don't approve of? Are you able to respect his different needs? Or is your big ego again there, just in the middle to block your view?

Let' give an example. A friend asks for some money. You may think that he needs to buy some food and when you see him buying a new pair of shoes you will most probably start criticizing him. Can you understand why? Because he did something against your expectations. He didn't lie to you. Your ego that knows everything misinterpreted it wrong. That's the point. To help others feel happy as they want and not let our ego make us feel upset. If you want to give him money, give him with all your heart. It's not your business to know his needs. If your ego stops you from felling happy for his new pair of shoes, don't give him any. And the reason you feel upset and lose energy is really silly. Because you can't see is point of view or because you wanted to be helpful without really feeling this way. Every time we decide to do something we must be fully conscious so that nothing can upset us and affect our disposition. Otherwise, you will try to move on by going backwards. We have already said that no condition beyond me should affect me. I don't expect good weather to make me feel happy. I don't need others to tell me if I am good or clever or pretty. That happened when I was young, before I got accustomed to my body and soul. Now, I must stand on my own feet and know which way to go. You need to love yourself and not be influenced by the rain. Think about it! What does the rain have to do with me? Why should a hateful look of my neighbor affect my day? If he feels happy that way, it has nothing to do with me. On the contrary, if I start talking about it, the problem gets bigger, I get involved, it affects me, I lose energy, I fill my heart with negative feelings and it finally becomes a bad habit to seek every negative act, beyond me to maneuver my mood. Don't get into this trap. If you love and respect yourself, you are the emperor of your mind, soul and body and let nobody spoil this inner peace

Mental energy motion

The movement of our mental energy is either progressive or reversible. We move progressively when we continually try to adjust to the environment. Humans have survived not because we were stronger or more important than other beings. We survived because we have the ability to adapt to the environment and the conditions we had to live in. If we think that we are the conquerors of this world, or we are the leaders of others and this arrogant belief remains firm and fixed, then wait for our collapse. It is like winning a prize once and stop trying harder. Social norms and media present popularity in a very attractive way and many people spend their whole lives trying to look like others and forget their uniqueness. When they achieve something great, they give up going further. I should not step on one of my successes and refuse to move forwards. The universe never stops moving. Can you think what will happen if a planet stopped moving for five minutes?

When our energy is reversible it is turned towards us. That means I want to escape from life. I keep myself to myself and deny facing reality. If you think deeper it is like desertion. Conservation is useful for a period of time. It is exactly the same as the foods in the fridge. We conserve them. But they won't last forever in the refrigerator. They will go off. And I find it amazing that we know when to throw off foods that have gone off but we have difficulty recognizing our inner beliefs that have gone off. As a conclusion reversibility is useful when we need to look deeply inside us. The purpose is not to be stuck to a permanent situation.

Being balanced means knowing when to move on progressively and when to choose reversibility. This is acquired by experience, by looking internally and interpreting the signs of my mood and happiness levels for one and the most major purpose. To protect myself and not let me exposed to conditions that may destroy my stability. In and out is the way we breathe as well. In and out is the way a baby is conceived. In and out is the law of existence. Let's comply with it, in order to breathe freely, in order to give birth to new blessed moments.

Suppose we need a glass of water. Whoever brings it to us he automatically gains a place in our heart. We regrd him as a very nice person who cares for us and does our favors. Can you see the mistake we make? We interpret this action as it suits us according to our narcissism levels. The same happens the other way round. I instantly have bad feelings towards the person who refuses to bring me the glass of water. I don't like him. I can't have tender feelings for him. Why? Both of my reactions are wrong. I only needed some water to drink, not to feed my narcissism, nor to start disliking someone. Here comes the question: How do I know who was sincere to me? How do I know that the one who satisfied my need acted out of the purest of motives and not because he wanted to make me feel obliged? Our big Ego is here again and never allows us to question actions that do not feed it. It is my ego who defines what a nice person means. We believe that good people are those who never say no to us. No, that's a great mistake we make and this way, we decrease our happiness levels. Everybody has the right to tell us no, if he believes so. Everybody has the right to disagree with us, as long as his aspect is well- supported. What others believe, what others do, what others say, have nothing to do with my disposition. I am the sun of my universe but let's not forget that others are also suns in their universe. The key is to coexist in harmony and not burn each other.

All these misinterpreted emotions lower my euphoria levels. You can easily understand that I see the tree and miss the forest.

But, what inner need grabs me from my hand and leads me to that wrong direction? In order the energy to move, there are two poles. If in the exterior environment there is only one pole, then the second has entered our unconscious mind. That is the reason we see some very kind and benevolent people having really mean feelings for others, or start behaving really awfully. Whatever is visible on one pole, there is exactly the opposite on the other one. That's why inner balance is significant.

Moderation in all things, even love or hate. They are the poles of the same energy battery. So, this power, moves beyond me, towards me, or has been enclosed in me. This is the problem. I don't feel the power that presses me because it compresses my energy. What we should achieve is to be balanced, and our energy should be aligned without ups and downs, so that we allow energy to light our halo.

Another misinterpreted emotion is when your son or friend talks badly to you. You don't react and you keep it inside you. You don't solve the problem this way. It is the energy you keep inside you. It is like a fire. If you don't let it go, it will bust out. This is very bad for us because we do harm to us. Epiphysis operates everything and when you are given the order you start shouting. That' a reason heart attacks and strokes happen. If you stuff your arteries with negativism and anger there is no need to wonder where this stroke came from.

You give the order to defend, out of fear of not knowing what will happen if you express your opinion and you keep it, and keep it and keep it. This way you open the door to depressive feelings to visit you. It is very important that you protect your body and soul every way you can. And the only way is by expressing your feelings. This is what you do during psychotherapy or confession. You express yourself and let anger and rage go away. Otherwise, they will keep getting greater and greater and it is impossible for you to control them. Then a sudden reaction of all these suppressed feelings is going to cause an explosion and reaction cannot be controlled. Don't choose to burn yourself. If others feel bad, it is their problem. If you see your house in flames, you won't think of your friend's which is safe. If you don't love yourself, there is no way of loving others.

You have to understand that no matter how long you keep negative feelings nest in your soul, the problem is not solved. This energy must move. The point is to decide which way to head it for. If it heads towards you, it will stay there. If it heads towards others you save you and burn others. The whole conscious mind must be trained so as to express it before the fire gets too big. Nobody must be burnt. Immediate action is needed so as to put this fire out.

You have to understand that you don't win anything, by pretending that you feel alright when you don't. Others can feel it whether you like them or not, but you keep it inside you and it hits you, and hits you, and you still do not react. Whether you tell it or not, your subconscious mind shows it. It is evident both to your words or actions because you are nervous and you don't speak or act with full consciousness. It is in your aura. You can feel it too when others are kind to you but you know they don't really like you. You are not the only one who can understand it. Others can feel it too when you act in a hypocritical way. Wonder why you don't express your real feelings. The longer it takes you to react, the fiercest your reaction will be. As soon as you realize the problem, tell them calmly if they have hurt you, if they have been unfair to you, but first be sure that your big ego is not there. Immediate action can save you from unnecessary pain. Thoughts give you energy. Whatever you do, you must do it with full consciousness. You can't ride a bike and look backwards. You will fall down. It is impossible for your mind to think of tomorrow and let your body think of now. You can't do something and expect other results. Full conscience of our thoughts, actions, and reactions is the key to achieve a balanced, happy inner self.

Steps that form our personality

Our personality is built step by step. First of all, we need to understand that we have access and we can conceive only three of our bodies. First comes our physical body. It is the body I can see, which takes us years to get familiar with. How many years does it take us to learn how to tie our shoelaces, or write or have a bath alone? We have forgotten how difficult it was for us to do things and most importantly we forget how hard we worked in order to fully use it. This is very didactic as we can understand that working hard leads to freedom

Then comes our sentimental body. We start making friends, having various relations; we get disappointed or disappoint others. That's the course of action in order to get familiar with our emotions. It also takes years to be able to recognize the people that suit me and most importantly the reasons they suit me.

Then follows our mental body. We go to school, to university and continue studying until we understand as much as we can. There are other bodies too, higher than those, but we don't have access to them easily. It is notable, that we can only see my physical body. We can see its shape and the room it takes up. What happens with our emotional and mental body? Our physiology does not have the organs to see them. We can't see to what extent they are spread. We can't understand how they are connected with other peoples' emotional or mental bodies.

As a result, we can infer that the spectrum we are able to see is really limited. It is only our ego that thinks that we are the most powerful beings on earth. We even believe that aliens will be like us. If their body mass is unconceivable for our physiology, how can we discern them? You can understand that we know almost nothing for ourselves, let alone cosmic influence.

The first step is to understand who you really are. Only then will you be able to form your personality which is the unity of our three conceivable bodies. Be sure that your soul will push you form a whole, strong and complete personality. How can your soul be expressed in an incomplete and weak personality?

The second step is to undertake the responsibilities of the people near you, your parents or your kids if they are unable to do it for themselves. The same applies to your job. Don't wait for others to do things for you if you can. Don't have the belief that everybody is like your mum to do you all your favors. You are a grown up now and you can do what you want for yourself. You will ask for help only if there is no way doing it yourself. I mean that, if we look for the easiest way because we cannot undertake our own responsibilities, we will never be complete personalities and every time others refuse to help us, we will get hurt. Offering is the greatest tactic as this way we will be able to receive as well. Do you remember action and reaction? Suppose I have two water melons in my hands and refuse to give them out of selfishness. Even it is raining watermelons I will not be able to get any if I insist on keeping the old ones which will get rotten and be thrown away. If this is not a negative egoism, what is it then?

When we become complete personalities, the third step is to influence others. Our halo brightens up and others can see it and gather around us. They want to unite with our positive view of life. This is exactly the way stars bright up. If you read about it, you will see that they work hard internally, by uniting 3 atoms producing this light which is visible to us. There are millions of stars that do not shine and nobody cares about them. Choose to be one of the brightest one. Only by working hard, uniting with people will we be able to shine. Then we will be those who will be able to brighten theirs too. If this isn't love, what is it then?

Nothing extraordinary was achieved with little effort. A strong personality has the power to influence billions of people. These strong personalities help evolution. Imagine what a better place this planet would be if all powerful people had allowed a good angel to lead them! That's why we must become strong and complete personalities. This way we will able to help evolution with good will and unselfish purpose. We all have souls which need to evolve but they are not expressed freely because of false beliefs and a great dose of egoism. We are only the centre of our own universe which shines and we can help others shine too so that our planet becomes a more luminous place.

Our unconscious part is our potential soul that needs to take the driver's seat. It is evolutionary to be able to let it sit at the driver's seat of our own vehicle. It is a very serious feat to let our soul express itself. The problem is when we think that no other drives better than us. We easily let our big ego drive us instead. The game is played to the extent we are able to prepare ourselves to help humanity progress. The more we are, the better and faster the evolution will take place. That's why we always have in mind that love brings love. The law of action and reaction becomes evident again. Let's start by loving ourselves so that our battery is filled and we can share some of our energy as well.

The three bodies we can perceive can help us when we believe there is no way out. There are days you go to work feeling tired. That means that your physical body suffers and is not in proper operation. You tend to excuse yourself by saying that you had not slept well the previous night. Suppose you are going to go on holiday and you had not slept at all the previous night because of your excitement. Most definitely you are not going to feel tired because your second body, the emotional body has taken over. The same situation has resulted in different outcomes. Both situations kept you awake. Going to work causes you to feel tired but visiting your favorite place makes you forget tiredness. You see that if we are careful and notice how your problems behave, it is easy to acquire the required knowledge in order to protect and respect ourselves.

This example shows that our positive emotional state can help overcome a problem our physical body faces. This is a first step of internal evolution. We see how the second body, our sentimental body can help solve a problem our first body faces. It is like a student and a teacher. We only need to work towards this realization by combining facts and events. This is the work needed to understand how my full body works. When I realize that the upper body of mine has this power, many of my problems can be solved.

The same applies to the connection of our emotional and mental body. Every problem is solved by the next one. To be more precise, when we have an emotional problem, we can solve it by using our mentality. Thinking logically without leaving emotional parameters to blur the distinction is going to lead me to the right solution. It is not a random fact that we have our brain. We must always bear in mind that walls raise when I build them myself. Every problem arises when I decide a situation should be defined as a problem. If I believe that nobody loves me, it is time my rational thought started working and gave me the answer.

Our physical body is grounded. We cannot see our sentimental body. We cannot perceive that it exists but it is what lights up. It is this feeling you have when someone approaches you. You may be attracted or repelled. This feeling is caused by the aura the other body transmits. Above it we have our mental body. Our thoughts create an invisible body. We all know that our thoughts can affect our body. To conclude, we must never forget that every physical pain, is solved by our emotional body and every sentimental problem is solved by our mental body. If we consciously notice the reason we feel hurt, it is easy to find the solution and stop abusing my body. Realization means freedom. Realization means knowing myself. Realization means loving myself!

Fear is the avoidance of pain

Many times we avoid doing things out of fear. Fear of losing, fear of being disappointed, fear of being cheated, fear of being hurt, and fear that we are not capable of doing what our soul longs for. Of course a thoughtful course of action is needed, but we lose thousands of happy moments out of the feeling that something will go wrong. I am sure that the words of you parents stroll on your mind. You hear them saying that this is not right, socially accepted, or does not meet the requirements of others, it is not proper, it is a certain failure and many more.

This is the first realization we have to detect its origins. Is it us or others who have made us be afraid to live the way you want? It is worth thinking back trying to remember what makes us be afraid of trying and doing things we wish. Is there a possibility that others' experiences have been passed on us? Of course it is not others' fault but the choice to embrace this fear was all yours now.

I define fear as the avoidance of pain. We fear that a situation will hurt us and this causes fear. What if I do not manage to succeed? What if I get hurt? What if I am not the winner? They have planted on my head that winning is the only way to feel happy. That's a real myth because the whole journey of trying will take me to the right destination which is collecting experience. Many of us can't see the positive side of going on that journey and many times we miss the beautiful view just because we will not be the first ones to reach the terminal. This happens because we are not ready to learn our lessons.

Society and media lead us to look up to people who are successful and rich. Nobody cares for the riches of my soul. What values most is not a pretty image or a full bank account with a soul full of unforgettable experiences. Beauty comes from deep inside you and it is evident in your aura, the way you live and the way you live. Beauty is part of you and can't hide if you do not cover it under misunderstood concepts. Next time you wish to seize the opportunity to get out of your comfort zone, think twice the view you deprive yourself of seeing.

Our brain games

I am going to put it as simple as possible. Our brain consists of three basic parts. The first part is the primary or reptilian brain which is the older part of our brain. The second is the emotional part which develops on top and the mental part, our logic, which is on the cortex.

All our fears are on the reptilian brain which is the part that controls instincts of animals. When you are in a situation of fear crisis this part comes out of you like a reptile. Like an animal. This is the reptile that some Saints try to tame. They don't want to kill it, but tame it, otherwise we will not develop and we are going to remain in a primitive level. This part governs us in difficult fearful or stressful situations and that's why they fight it, in order not to let it beat us. It is surely useful but not from the post of the governor. It is connected to our primitive instincts and it is more intense during childhood.

While we are angry, we tend to threat others and say things that we could not even imagine. This means that your reptilian brain has taken control over your sentimental or logical part.

Some of the results of not having control over this part of our brain is because we are superstitious. Many people have connected some situations with the result. For example if ones wife sits next to them when their favorite team lost, it is more likely that he will never let her sit next to him during the championship. They believe that she was responsible their team did not manage to win. Is there any chance that a team will never lose?

The cause precedes the result and this is part of the reptilian brain. Everybody who is superstitious acts the same way. You see coaches who wear the same caps or T-shirts during important matches. The cause precedes and the result comes afterwards.

Our aim is to help humanity evolve but until we realize that we must know the way to help ourselves evolve this will be a very difficult procedure. Only until we learn what causes negativity and what prevents us from having full conscience of our actions, emotions and thoughts, we will not be afraid to step of our souls footsteps. Then it is a matter of time for humanity to be in the right orbit of evolution.

Evolution is not only the advancement of high technology. Love and forgiveness were taught thousands of years ago and we are still unable to understand their meanings let alone live by following them. Following their rules and laws is a conscious procedure, which needs work and not just words.

You are the governor of yourself

Nobody has the power to affect the balance and peaceful flow of your bodies unless you permit it. Self-suggestion is a very important step. It is up to you if it becomes a very useful or self-destructive tool. If you learn how this mechanism works then you will know exactly what to do, and this will not confuse your wishes with all the "must do" others have passed on you.

We must unite our unconscious with our conscious mind. Unity brings happiness, satisfaction and you are closer to self-realization. Remember the atoms in stars that produce their brilliance. The unity of the conscious and unconscious mind will show us the reason why we do, say, believe and react the way we do. Work is needed to be done in order to reach the point of using our whole complete mind. Consequences will come whether you like it or not. Be sure to enjoy them and stop blaming destiny. Nothing happens at random, no sign is accidental. Being genius means combining things and understanding as many signs as possible.

You must learn to be aligned with the cosmic energy and realize that you are synchronized with everything around you, so close and so distant at the same time. You must be aligned with everything that exists, because everything out there is connected. If you don't accept this aspect, pain and hurt feelings will devour your wishes, your subsistence and no matter how many years will pass you will still try to find the meaning of life.

Moving our hands without thinking about it, closing our eyes when we want, step forwards when we wish, means we have become accustomed to our physical body. These expropriations need to be conquered by our emotional and mental bodies. Only then will we able to fully enjoy the presence of our existence, as we must never forget that neither our existence is random.

When someone is grounded to his natural body, all his thoughts revolve around money, sex and material things. He is going to pray to our creator for a girlfriend or winning the lottery. Is this the meaning of the evolution of life? Of course not. This is the lowest part of Maslow pyramid. The belief that money and sex are the basic elements of happiness, keeps us down to the basis of the pyramid and the path we have to follow is long and steep.

If we realize our mistake, we must develop our emotional body. Then we are going to ask others to love us. When we are hurt emotionally and all our problems are of emotional nature, it is time we learned to use our mental body. The unity and alignment of these invisible parts of us will bring us closer to real light. Otherwise you feel you go into a black hole and real light becomes more distant. Our planet has light and have you ever wondered why? The whole universe is black but we see it blue. This is the truth. Sea is blue but as much sea you take home, it will never be blue. It is up to us to see the light inside us or remain trapped in our black hole. The choice is exclusively ours.

The only way we can reach the level of being balanced is to fight with our inner self. Real balance comes only after a conscious fight whether it concerns countries, friendships or yourself. The law is the same. It is difficult because it is painful, and as we have said we avoid pain out of fear. Only by fighting can we find the point of stability and harmonization. We need to express our inner thoughts, to collide with everything others led us to believe in order to find true balance. It does not mean that others always want to make us break up with our inner self. This is what we know, this is what we have been doing for years and nobody showed us the other way. The difference is that we know now, and we can help others as well.

We have to listen carefully to what others tell us and judge what we hear, and decide as a unity, using our emotional and mental part of us on equal doses. Results may come as a shock to us and knock down the beliefs we had adopted up to now. We must not fear of this shock. It is the healthiest thing we can offer ourselves. It is what saves us from going towards the wrong direction, leading us to real balance. We may get hurt by realizing the illusion of fixed ideas, fears, and tactics but this is the way out. Only after facing this collision and fight will we be able to readjust ourselves. Otherwise, we live in a fragile bubble with the fear of breaking at any time. This fear will bring about stress, anxiety, misery and of course disease. Is this the life we want to live? Is this the reason we were born? Of course not.

Everything we hide inside us is what keeps us apart from uniting our inner part with real love. Since we were kids everybody has been telling us what is right and what is wrong. We are used to listening to others and not our self. I don't think it is logical, because we have been given a unique brain, a unique soul and our job is to unite them. It has nothing to do with right or wrong, good or bad. It has to do with understanding and uniting. Whatever takes me out of my comfort zone; it is automatically regarded as bad. Who defined bad and good? Who told me that there is only one way to proceed? What is good for me may look bad for somebody else. Dividing ourselves helps us only to keep a greater distance from our soul. That is the work needed to be done with absolute conscience. Clearing out the vision in front of me and getting rid of everything that blurs my view is our power and liberty. The choice to open my shattered windows is exclusively mine.

Love vs Ego

Our bodies constitute a whole universe which is one of a kind. We must feel great gratitude to our body for every single operation it does in order to keep us alive. We must feel blessed our eyes can see, our body supports us, our mind can think, our stomach digests and so on. The way to the truth is long and twisted. Bit by bit, step by step we can reach real light which is hidden inside us. We need to advance our conscience and realize that our skin is only what others see, but under it, billions of cells work for us. That's what keeps us alive, healthy, happy and complete. Do not be cruel to your hidden helpers because if they make a revolution, you will have to double the conscience and effort just to reach to the point you were before. Pain and struggle just go to our previous condition. How much energy will you spend for nothing?

All roads lead to Rome. Roma! If you read it backwards it forms the word Amor, Love! You don't understand it but every step you make you open a new path. Disease is not the only road to follow. You only need to take the right turning once regardless of your previous choices. The proper turning has to be taken just once even if you have made thousands of mistakes before. They were the lessons you had to learn. Don't feel sorry for your mistakes but feel blessed they were the brightest moments because they led you to a new reality where you are wiser and more conscious.

The difference between the destiny of our soul and all the "musts" that have curved your personality leads to collision between our conscious and our unconscious mind. Our soul pushes us and our personality refuses to follow. Can you understand how many everyday fights you have to face? What we really need is not what others led us to believe I needed. We end up spending a whole life trying to earn more and more money, because they have taught us that money brings happiness, only to realize that I have spent the best years of my life for a vain purpose. Nobody taught me about moderation nor did I look for it. Our respiratory system shows how things work. We need a certain amount of oxygen in order to survive and in order to inhale we first need to exhale. Our body tells us clearly what we need to do. Firstly, we need a certain amount of everything as two bottles of oxygen in your lungs would only harm you. The second lesson is that if we do not throw away the old belief, there is no room for the new one.

Working towards understanding ourselves is essential and the only way to advance and gain experience. The dilemma is not which way to follow, which career better suits me, which profile would make me more acceptable but when we ignore our soul whispering to us. The right way is to listen to our inner self, respect it, embrace it and love it.

When you reach the level others expected from you, then you are going to feel distressed for all the things you sacrificed. Pain comes to remind you that your souls know better than those around you. It is never too late to realize your misunderstanding and put it right. This way you start going up the stairs to meet with your real self and love you unconditionally.

You have to bear in mind that nothing special has been easy. Listen to your soul, your intuition and trust them. They know you better than anybody else. Others like playing with our minds and this is what stress does as well. Suppose you want to talk to someone and express your disappointment of something he did, but you just look at him crossing the room without being able to say a word because many thoughts block you from expressing yourself. Your cells, your soul feels betrayed. How long will they tolerate you treating them as if they don't exist? Don't wait for them to take care of you if you ignore them. You miss the chance to show your inner part of you that you are allies but your personality traits keep you back and the message sent inside you is that you are opponents. The moment he goes out of the room, it is the moment you start feeling bad. Feeling bad with whom? Him? Of course not. You had the chance, your soul showed you the way but you refused to follow it. Realize that everything is up to you and stop nagging and protesting. This tactic leads nowhere.

Another awkward moment is when we are with someone who knows more than us. Our ego does not let us accept that others are somehow better. We have difficulty in telling that we don't know, or that we want to learn from him, because we see it as an imperfection we want to hide. We can't understand that I lose the chance to go to a more advanced level due to our big ego! This may happen because our mum used to tell us that we are the best or the cleverest students, although she was willing to do our homework for us. This is a game our mind plays to us. The right answer is to listen. How else will you learn? Accept the fact that you are not Mr all-knowing and stop thinking how you can show something beyond you, something more than what you are.

Everybody is important and valuable in this life but not everybody does it the same way. Stop thinking where to throw your arrows. The best archers were the Amazons while riding on their horse, because they had no time to think and focus on the targets. The let their instinct and soul lead their arrows.

Think of four people sitting in the same room. If you ask them to describe the room, their descriptions will be totally different because they see a different aspect of the room. Everyone has his own aspect of life and it is his truth. This is not the problem as you start working. Change your seat, turn your head around, acquire a more spherical view of the room. You will realize that everybody describes his own truth. When you see the whole room, though, you can decide where to place your chair and see what pleases you. The procedure has just started and it only takes a harmless motive and work to discover your inner needs, the needs your soul try to show you.

Looking at your inner self is very important. Open your doors. The doors of your soul ought to be open so as to let new ideas come into your mind. We have to learn the mechanisms that keep us apart from our real self. If someone tells me something that upsets me, it means that I discovered something I refused to see on me. In other words, he is my mirror. We are all mirrors until we decide to look deeply in ourselves with the eyes of our hidden soul and not through the eyes of others. If I feel insulted, it automatically means I feel guilty someway. The word guilt in Greek is enohi coming from en – eho which means "have in me". Actually, the Greek language hides a hidden fortune waiting to emerge.

I am going to give you a very explicit example. If someone glowers at you, you automatically stop liking him. Can you understand the work you have to do with yourself in order to stop being affected by the way someone looks at you? Only *you* are the one who gives others the power to control your feelings and your mood. If your child or a person you really love glowers at you, you are not going to stop loving him. How strange you let someone influence you and others not in the same situation! You need to work internally so as to reach to a point that nobody affects you. Love makes the difference! Real love does not let your ego affect your disposition. You may well start thinking that loving others will save you! Oh! Don't forget to lock the door so that you your big ego cannot enter this time.

Another mistaken belief due to our ego is that we want things or people just for us. I want our mum to be mine, our house to be mine, money, my granny, my husband and so on. Why is that? Why others can't have a share? These beliefs make me feel falsely safe and I become the most delicious food for my ego. Is this ever possible? How can my mum belong only to me? She is another unique universe who took over the responsibility to bring me up and do her best for me. Do I own her? I encroach her existence. Is your wife a table or a packet of cigarettes you bought? Why should you consider yourself the main owner of her? You can understand now that our ego drives us backwards and keeps us prisoners by locking the doors of our mind with double locks.

If my mum loves my siblings too, which is pretty fair, it does not mean that she does not love me. Love is energy and there is plenty of it out there. The problem is that we polarize it through the negative pole of our ego and we lose all the magic. I respect my wife and I am faithful to her for as long as we are together. It may be forever, and may not. The same applies to my husband. Everyone is a unique soul of this infinite bright star dust and it is a pity to keep it locked in a bottle. This is pure selfishness! This holds me back because I think that only this bottle is valuable, while the boundless macrocosm is full of love! The fact that I am not willing to open my soul's eyes makes me a selfish egoist. I have just ordered my happiness levels to go back to the bottom and never come back.

Understanding how our ego works will help us advance, step forwards, open the windows of my soul to let fresh air come in, and feel free to remember the purpose we were born for. Love everything around you, love and understand everyone around you. They want to show you the way to uncover every buried flow so that your soul is so bright that the sun is jealous of you!

Unchain yourself

The first factor that keeps you chained and does not allow you to move on is fear. I am afraid not to disobey orders, I am afraid in case I don't handle well a situation, I am afraid that something bad will happen to those I love. Evil always tries to make you unable to unchain your legs and step forward in order to find light. In addition, not only does it prevent you from developing and reaching light, but it also steals your resources. This keeps you back, it delays you, it makes your battery reach low levels and as a consequence, you are out of energy.

When fear occupies the seat on your brain, evil will try to keep you chained with guilt. I feel guilty if I go to a funeral and can't cry. I feel guilty because everybody cries, and so should I. Otherwise, others will judge me as an apathetic person, someone who lacks human feelings. It leaves no room for another aspect concerning life and death. Who does that? I was not born with this belief. Evil can't produce light and tries to steal from those who have. It takes your light because it does not have any. How can someone who has no light show up? By stealing yours. Funerals are the Promised Land of evil because there are many people gathered together who are in pain and cry. Thus, evil steals your light and comes ahead. However, I should never forget that it was me who permitted this to happen.

The third chain is fear. Many times we feel guilty because of social norms. Imagine you do things that are against the general public opinion. For example, I am afraid to tell someone that I like him straightforward because they will think I am being immoral. Our creator did not mean to make us feel guilty. If someone plants guilt inside you, this is evil, not good. If good makes you fearful, what will evil do then? Free you? Of course not. So, every time you feel fear or guilt try to find who implanted these fixed beliefs in your mind.

There are many things that may cause guilt feelings. Let's take the example that you stand up for yourself and this displeases someone else, the case where you tell someone the truth which is not what suits him, the instance that you decide not to do what others expect from you, the times you try to prove you are not an elephant and get out of control and may raise your voice to someone you shouldn't have. Not to mention the times you did not please others' wishes. All these situations make you feel guilty and this feeling is your energy thief. You compromise and you do not express yourself. Don't forget that all this suppression will find its way out in a way you are not going to like.

Loving ourselves means being faithful to us, our wishes, our soul, our destiny, no matter what. Our aim is to be tuned according to our vibrations and not others. Otherwise, shaking will make us feel sick until we decide to vomit and get rid of everything that does not agree with us. Loving myself means having faith to our Creator, accepting all the talents He has given us, enriching them, feeling full and blessed. Fear and guilt has nothing to do with us. We don't want them to block us, to hold us back, and that's why we should decide to continue this magic journey without them. It is our decision to eliminate any extra burden on our back!

When you overcome guilt, the next part of the chain is desire which takes over. Do material things attract you? You sacrifice everything to acquire them! Where is your happiness hidden? In a car, a man, a woman, a house, or a better car, a better man, a more beautiful woman, a bigger house than your neighbor? After some time, when you get used to all these achievements or belongings you may realize that your happiness levels are much lower. True happiness is a long way away. Who fooled you? Nobody but yourself just because you let your fear and false desire sneak in you. You fear that that if your car is not be as modern as others', your wife is not be as pretty as your friend's, you house is not as luxurious as your colleagues'', you husband is not as successful as your parents told you deserve, you will be a loser. Now you blame society, your nerves do not let you enjoy your every moment to the full, you think that the only thing you managed to do is beat the wind that is, nothing. It was all your choice. You did it and think twice before you continue to allow this pain chain to keep you imprisoned.

You have to talk with yourself, but remember to be kind with you, not only with others, try to understand you, to find your inner motive that lets desire maneuver your life. Why do you want certain things? Are you happier when you own them or when you show them? Try to think deeper and decide what really makes you happy, what touches your soul, what advances your energy levels. The more you revolve around others, the darker your inner self will get. Discover your own light, and be self- illuminated. Dark will never find you and more importantly nobody else can deprive you of your inner shine!

The next step after desire takes over is felling obliged to third parties, not to yourself. Have you ever wondered who that third party is when you sign contracts? I am the first party, you are the third, who is the second party and you hide it? If I must be obliged to the other I should have said that I am obliged to second parties. Who is hidden behind the second party? Certainly not the good will. Good wants you happy and balanced and not distressed. You start feeling obliged to people you love. You feel obliged to your parents who raised you, obliged to your boss who pays you, obliged to your friend who listens to you, even obliged to your partner who lives with you. Where is your participation? Don't you offer anything? Why do you close your eyes and can't see that you gave your parents the chance to experience this great love from you, the responsibilities they took and became wiser, and the many hours you work productively in order your boss to be richer? Is marriage or cohabitation an obligation? Isn't the pure unity of two bodies who decide to live one next to the other? What blocks you from seeing all those things you do and offer to others? If helping does not make you blessed, what will? Fear, guilt, desire or obligation? You can see how wrong this is from the beginning.

Stop and think how many women suffer in their marriage and do not dare think to divorce for the sake of their kids. They think that those poor children will feel unhappy and depressed. Have you ever thought what you teach your kids? You teach them to suffer everything in order not to free themselves. This aspect is difficult to be understandable because we need to reverse our way of thinking. As we have said, change brings freedom.

Those four stages are responsible for not letting you find authentic freedom. Fear, guilt, desire, obligation should disappear if you want to free yourselves and enjoy the full benefits of life. Understanding how they work will show you the way to remove them from your way One by one, step by step in order not to lose your light, your energy. Our aim is to fill ourselves with energy and not lose it.

Orienting energy

Everything in our daily life shows us the way. We need to be observant of everything that happens around us. Think of electricity. Although this energy has existed for centuries and was all around us, we were able to turn on the light only when we managed to orientate this energy through cables. It took centuries and a lot of work. The same law applies to humans, as we are energy, we are power and light. Our aim is to orientate this energy in the inner part of our souls in order to turn on our inner light. Orientation of our wishes and our goals is the way to get away from the darkness we are in, and fill with the power of light we have buried deep inside us.

Our purpose is not to waste our energy resources, our light but to gather it. Having surplus resources gets us closer to our Creator. So, you will not be afraid even of death. Who is afraid of death? Those who have less amount of energy than when they were born. Those who have not lived their lives as their soul wished. Those who have lived in accordance to their vibrations, are not afraid and enjoy their life because they have managed to save energy and they know that having more energy since when they were born is the key to happiness and fulfillment.

Let's give an example. If when I came to this world I had 100 watt and I have lost a considerable amount of it because of the various misunderstandings and have only 60 or 50 Watt, I don't want to leave this world because inwardly I know that instead of approaching the big great light, I moved further away and now I have to work harder in order to shorten the distance. I secretly realize that my final destination is more difficult to reach. The sooner you realize it, the quicker you stabilize it.

A way to understand if someone has enjoyed his life is to see if he is afraid of death or not. When I get nearer to the big light I feel safe. Some cultures believe that crying for the deceased is an insult because you think that he has gone the other way, he has gone with less energy, and he is far away from his destination. Instead they celebrate death because their beloved one has gone nearer to the great light. They are not wrong. For many, death is a very painful and difficult situation to cope with as our sentiments take over. Our sentiments are like water. A slight shaking can blur it.

Sometimes you feel awkward when you are with certain people. You keep yourself to yourself because you feel they notice every movement you do or every word you say. You may have a headache after you meet them. I call these people energy thieves or better energy zombies. They have lost all their energy and unconsciously they try to steal yours. They don't do it consciously, but that's how their defense system works. The problem is not them, but you. You allow them to enter our house and take whatever they want. Would you do that with your personal belongings? I don't think so. So, why do you allow it to happen to your driving force?

Who or what is responsible for our losing energy instead of multiplying it and orientate it? Many fixed convictions that have been passed from generation to generation. Of course, these convictions change from a place to another or from one era to another. Think of some cultures how they treat women, the value of education, the freedom to express themselves, the virtue of maintaining their soul happy. Wherever we live, however we have been brought up, regardless of our social class, race and income we ought to be faithful to us, to respect us and love us. Happiness, love and balance come from inside and not in reverse.

Counterbalance theory

The counterbalance theory applies to many scientific fields. It works like a thermostat. A very simple definition is when a reason creates the result, and the result affects the reason. Let's put it more analytically. What does a thermostat do? It makes the heater start working, so it is the reason that the room becomes warmer. As soon as the room reaches the desired temperature, the thermostat goes off. The result of the reason, which is the thermostat, affects again the result and puts the heater off.

The same applies to our body. When it is hot, we sweat in order to cool the temperature of my body and when this is achieved I reach my previous temperature levels. A reason and a result counterbalance in order to reach the initial temperature. This is called cybernetics in mathematics.

Let's give another simple example. It is when voters vote for a government. A decision of the Prime Minister will affect voters. So the reason and the result are not univocal. I vote for someone and his decision affects me.

The same applies to dreaming. You have a reason, a bottled-up feeling which appears in your dream in order counterbalance, to start working so that it does not come out as a shock to you.

If someone insults me by telling that I am silly, he activates my thermostat. I am in a state of a shock. I start working how to overcome this insult. I actually don't know what to do or how to do it, but counterbalance is already triggered.

The same happens to our brain after a shock such as a divorce, disease, death. This shock brings a counterbalance to my whole entity, which tries to keep me in balance to the new conditions. It is a mechanism that will help you adapt to the new situation. A reason brings a result, and this result affects the reason.

Our purpose is to find balance by understanding all the freedom of mind that has been wrongly repelled. Our subconscious mind takes all the apperceptions and forms them as it suits it. A good example of it is what we dream of. Our dreams are way different to what people dreamt of two thousand years ago. They would most probably dream of antelopes or deer. There is no way that people back then, would have an image of a mobile phone in their dreams. The apperceptions are different but the result is the same. Your subconscious mind transforms them as it is more suitable for it.

The way that our brain and body work is very important to be understood. This way it is easy to understand why we feel badly or react in a certain way to a certain situation. When we learn how the mechanism of our body works, it is easy to hit the core of the problem. Knowing the mechanism is like knowing the solution to the problem.

Work with yourself

Everyone has to save himself by working with ourselves. This is the way to find true freedom, collect energy and save your soul. It is a procedure that has to be done by you. Any way it suits you. It is like learning playing a musical instrument. Nobody cares the way you learn how to play it, whether you have private lessons, or go to music school or you are self taught. The result is that counts. When you are invited to play in the big orchestra of humanity, you must be an expert without producing discordance. All roads lead to Rome, you have to follow the one that suits you but do it with full consciousness to get to your destination.

So, all the work has to be done by you. If you are lazy to work for yourself, nobody would ever bother to do it for you and you leave the door open to allow evil enter. If evil will intervenes, it does not mean that it does the work of good will. The longer it takes you to understand how it works, the longer and more it will hurt you. The victory of your unconscious mind is a matter of time. The choice of how much pain you want to feel, is yours.

Our unconscious mind is what unites us, not separates us. It is the fifth essence, the ether that unites us all. But it is worth noting how they try to make us fear of others. We regard them as opponents, as competitors, or even enemies. There will always be a pretext or a reason to keep us in distance. Either he smells, or is poor, or different, or short, or very rich, whatever. An excuse to keep us apart is always present. Can someone separate the sky above our heads? Do not forget stars. The more atoms they unite, the brighter they shine.

We need to overcome and change all the beliefs that keep us trapped and chained. It is not easy, but it is not impossible. It needs work and faith in your powers. You need to get rid of all the small – sized clothes that dressed you with. Do not let sentiments avert you from choosing the right size yourself. Choose what to wear according to your own style and taste. You are a grown up now and you have the ability to use your voice, for your own comfort, your own euphoria. Suppose you are thirty and refuse to change your baby clothes. You obviously feel uncomfortable as you can't move easily. You feel tight and trapped. It is a cacophony. It is like tuning your guitar according to your mum's instructions who knows how to tune her trumpet. Cacophony again. So once again, the choice is only yours. Your freedom and power depend on how hard you work with yourself, how seriously you listen to yourself, how faithful are to yourself, how well you know yourself, so as to love yourself.

Lets' not be unfair with fear. It has its positive side as well. Its cause makes the difference. I mean that fear also makes us move. When we choose not to move is destructive. When we can't move is disastrous for us. Think of people who are confined to a bed and can't move. Their back "leaks". Think of the planets! Can you imagine what will happen if they stop moving? Chaos. Everything is in constant motion and this should be teaching us that we must never stop evolving. We should stop being pathetic to what is happening around us. They all show us the right direction.

The moments that seem to be the most difficult externally are those that tell us that this is our chance to move. The chance to adapt to the new situation in order to break down this barrier and go on to understand what is this gift given to us. How else can we change and get rid of what it hurts us? Otherwise, you are stuck and suffer. This is the point we falsely start feeling unlucky and that the whole universe, society, people are against us. The only course of action is to work in order to find your new balance! What seems bad is what it takes you out of your comfort zone and tells you to proceed. If you don't want to move, your fate is not to blame. Who is to blame? Just you. Your way of thinking that you are the center of the universe and everything turns around you misdirect you. That's egoism and lack of knowledge. That's what holds you back. That's your decision to leave your door wide open to intruders. It's you who allow it to happen according to your will. How ironical you never leave the door of your house wide open to intruders! Once again, we can't realize how many things we choose to suffer and then blame others!

If you wait for good luck to come and get you out of difficult times, you are totally mistaken. Luck is depicted as a deaf, blind and lunatic lady stepping on a round stone. The round stone symbolizes that she is unstable and you cannot trust her. The fact that she is characterized as blind and deaf and lunatic shows us that she does not know who she gives luck to, she does not listen to your desires, and she does not know what she does. She may give you what you need one day, but she may take them from you the next day. So, relying on luck is a false belief that the only thing it manages to achieve, is to make you stop working and wait in vain. Don't forget that waiting means not proceeding! It creates a false belief that an external power will save you, and this happens because you don't believe in your own power.

We need to concentrate our thoughts, either by praying or meditating or any way you can do it. It is the same process as electricity is the concentration of energy in cables. It is the same process that leads us to discover our inner light. In other words, do not waste your thoughts, words, actions aimlessly. A torn cable cannot transmit electricity.

The levels of energy we receive should be increasing. We need to prepare ourselves in order to bear these new added levels so that we can be aligned and not burnt. We must be prepared to welcome this energy and manage to make use of it. It is like weightlifting. If I can lift fifty kilos, I need to train myself in order to be able to lift eighty kilos without hurting my muscles or my back. In our every aspect of life, in every achievement, work and conscious adaptation are the basic ingredients of a good life's recipe.

Our checkpoints in order to understand reality are our five senses. It is common sense that our five senses are fallacy. What I mean is that our eyes can see certain frequencies. We can't see beyond red, the infrared beams, nor beyond violet, the ultraviolet beans of light. So, this simple ascertainment makes me realize that my senses are deceitful. None of my senses enable me to see or perceive viruses, but they are here. What we feel is fallacy. Our reality is fallacy. The same applies to my ears as I can't hear all the noises that exist around me.

This is the work of the brain. In order to protect itself and get into the reality others define for it, it must compromise. Knowing reality makes us conscious of our existence and this consciousness leads to our ability to get to know and love ourselves. It is not only about what we lack but about what we have and go unnoticed. We have more powers than we realize, and just because we are not consciously aware of them, we are not able to use the unknown ones. All this happens, because we take everything for granted and do not work towards realization. The more we insist on closing our eyes the more we delay to witness light.

As we have analyzed before, we have three bodied we can perceive. For example, I may have an apple (physical), I may eat it because you offered it to me and I have to be kind to you (sentimental). We use our intellect when I think if I want to eat it and why I want to eat it. Our eyes and voice help us express our emotions. Wide open eyes with no voice means feelings of shame. This means that our body knows well how to transmit emotions. You don't need to tell me that you are ashamed, because I can see it and behave in accordance to my ethic codes.

Work with your eyes open, with your voice sounding and your hands giving. This applies from medicine to sex. My aim is to give you the stimulus to have access to a higher level of understanding yourself and reach the point of loving yourself.

In order to love myself, I need to know how the mechanisms of our three bodies work. For example, if a bad thought prevents me from keeping aligned and balanced with the cosmic energy, I must be aware of the mechanisms and get rid of them. If I can't solve a big problem I have, I have to use my mental body consciously and transfer my thoughts to the point I did not have this problem, let's say, think of my holidays. I transfer my thought to a situation that this problem did not trouble me and did not even exist. We have to be fully conscious if I truly want to stop thinking about this problem, or else having something to worry about becomes a permanent habit. Many times, our mind keeps us troubled in order not to use its power to control us. It is the way I tune it. The choice is again exclusively mine.

Helping others

Our desire, many times, is directly associated with others without us being able to understand it because we omitted self- searching to pinpoint our real motives. Why do I help others? Is it because I really feel like it, or because I want to see their gratitude towards me in their eyes? Is it a true sense of helping or do I want to be a hero in the eyes of others'? Here, consciousness and introspection have an important role to play. There are two possible reasons.

One reason is to be kind and helpful to others because I hear my inner need calling me. This gives me great pleasure and advances my happiness levels. In this case I refill my battery with energy and feel useful. It is a reflection of my soul towards others. In this case, I don't feel the need to show off or expect others to thank me. I help others because I really feel like it and what others feel does not affect me. I just do what my soul asks for.

In the case I choose to be helpful because I have a strong wish to feed my ego with the pity of others. If I expect for their gratitude or my subconscious wish is to make them feel obliged to me the game is lost. My inner drive is not being supportive but I have just fed my great ego. In this case, I will probably start telling others about my great act of helping or giving just to hear from others how good I am.

To take it further, we can identify this is happening when people help others and don't stop telling about it. They inform everybody of their acts of kindness out of the need to feel important and heroes. They help because they are driven by the will to show off their actions. Others help because they know that their happiness levels increase because of their act and they do it in silence. You can understand how close and how different these beliefs are at the same time.

It is also possible for things to get worse if the result is not the one I expect. What I mean is the case I give some money to a friend, expecting that he lacks the necessary food supplies. If I see him in a restaurant I will most possibly feel betrayed and blame my good heart for being fooled. Do you know why? Because my ego led me define his need. If his need is different from what I imagined I feel deceived because we firmly believe that others ought to think, feel and act the way we do. What a pity, and what a common fallacy to think I am the one who knows everything and my beliefs are the correct ones. I just deprive others of the right to have their personality.

I may also start criticizing him to mutual friends that he does not budget his money well or for delaying giving my money back. Now, my battery levels reach the bottom. Instead of an act of kindness, it turns out an act of bad will. If we analyze it from energy levels aspect, it is easy to see that my act of kindness would earn me some watt but talking behind my friends back and criticizing her, costs me many watts without realizing it. Instead of gathering energy, I waste it and this loss becomes my enemy. And all this happens for the simple reason that I did not take my decision to lend her money consciously. I should have given her so much as not to care when she is going to repay me and understand that her own needs had nothing to do with me. I should not have let my ego made me jump to conclusions for others' needs.

Consciousness is demanded to determine what my purpose is. Either I feel the need to help and do it, or I don't feel this need and I don't do it. It is of crucial importance to realize if my act is a self-serving attitude or not. If I really wish to be supportive or reproduce my ego, if I want to gather or lose energy, are decisions that should be very consciously taken. The reason beggars are ragged and always sit down when they beg for money is to give you the impression you are at a higher level than them so as you feel more important. They just feed your ego as you feel superior and consider you are in a more advantageous and favorable position. If a well dressed person, taller than you begged for money, you would definitely refuse to give even a pence. Inwardly, you feel inferior and your benevolent nature decides to abandon you.

As you can see incidents that escape our realization may be energy loss factors. They are not directly understood but they preoccupy your subconscious part of your brain. The fact that your friend went to a restaurant with the money you lent her may keep you awake all night as you most probably magnify this incident by remembering every minor trait of her that could have annoyed you. Your mind amplifies your misunderstanding and instead of feeling blessed you feel ill-fated. It is time we got away from this vicious circle and found our bright human nature that gives us reasons to love ourselves.

The whole game is played by unchaining yourself from the vicious circle of the snake eating its tail and advancing level. This will lead you to another spectrum where you feel able to breathe freely and get rid of every suffocating condition and belief. In order to advance and evolve, you need to work with yourself. You need to do it by yourself and not wait from fate, luck or any other external help to take you there.

Consciousness is needed in order to be able to ascent to a higher level alone. You have to realize that this is the only way to protect yourself from the disastrous impacts on you. The only thing you must do, is stop being lazy, waiting for manna from heaven. Everything in this universe is revolving nonstop for centuries. There is no other way to find balance. Discover what prevents you from allowing your sun to be as bright as it deserves.

Not being able to know your strengths and weaknesses you run the risk of taking the wrong path which leads nowhere. It may be part of the procedure to find real purpose but the earlier you realize that you are in the wrong way, the earlier you can find the right one. The one that will take you to the right objective. The purpose of our mind is not to block us or think of everything we consider "bad", but with the right tuning we can make full use of its power and turn it to precious tool to free ourselves from every day minor worries or misunderstandings.

This has a practical application to the field of choosing a job. You see that an acquaintance of yours is a successful insurance consultant. You envy his life, you want to possess his car, and travel to all the places he has gone. Without knowing his background, all the work, studies and problems he had to overcome, you believe that you can do the same by wearing his suit and carry his briefcase. Can you imagine the results when the desired outcome will not meet your expectances? You will feel a loser, that people are insane and do not appreciate your efforts, or blame your acquaintance that he deceives his clients. What you missed is the question whether you are suited to this job. Your decision to follow this career was not out of love to help your clients but to take advantage of them in order to have access to material possessions you thought would bring you happiness.

Why put yourself in that situation? Because without realizing it you saw the external image of him, his house and car and you did not bother to work. You can't realize that it was you the one who wanted to deceive others. Don't stand still and watch the lives of others. Start working with yourself, discover your talents, improve your knowledge, and the elevator to take you to the upper floor will be waiting for you with its doors open. Only then a whole world of prospects will be open in front of you. Laziness will keep you on the ground floor and look at what is going on around you. Watching others going up is not the solution. Only by choosing to be a part of this world, offering your little stone to humanity, will you feel complete and satisfied. Only then will you be able to realize the reason you were born and the purpose you have chosen to execute so as to help humanity. You have to choose if you want to be an outsider or a welcome guest! Once again, realization is freedom!

Catharsis

When you face a problem or a cul-de-sac, it is like discovering a small stain on the wall of your living room. You get the right tools and start cleaning it. When this spot is cleaned the rest of the wall looks ugly because you realize that it is even dirtier. When you paint the whole wall, you see the difference with the next room and you start painting the other room too. Afterwards, you see the difference with the doors and you start cleaning them as well. In fact, you end up to a renovation and it all started from a small stain. You have a clean house now and it was achieved by hard work.

As you can understand, every stain, every problem needs work to clean it up. Ask why, and the relation it has with you. For example, do not stick to the problem, but to the chance it opens up in front of you. Break the outer shell, and move on. Don't be afraid of change. Everything has a reason to happen and you ought to find the internal message every situation sends you. Clean yourself from all the disbeliefs that make your soul dirty.

If change knocks on the door and sometimes it may become quite violently, stop and think. Why is this happening to me? What is the hidden message I haven't understood? Think of the lockdown period when many people could not stand staying at home. If we think deeper, we will see that it was the same destiny that gave me my freedom, and the same destiny takes it from me. It has nothing to do with good and bad. It is the same law. Let's wonder if I maltreated my freedom. Can you remember yourself complaining that you have no time to enjoy your family or the coziness of your house? I can't say it is good when it suits me and bad when it takes me out of my comfort zone. Look at the chance that is in front of you. The chance you are given to spend more time with your family, the chance to get to know yourself. How do you behave to yourself? If this looks tiring to you, reconsider the way you talk and behave to yourself. Are you kind with yourself? Do you scold yourself? Do you criticize yourself? Do you argue with yourself? Are you friendly or unfriendly with yourself? Try to get to the root of the problem, and don't stick to the superficial cause.

Everything that happens around us is a message sent to our soul. If we start being observant and see the internal side of this message we can then understand what we say and do unconsciously. Many times we even repeat misery words, attitudes or practices of others. This encloses me in a circle that prevents me from breathing. However, if you turn this exterior stimulus towards you and ask kindly to yourself why the certain situation affected you, why you felt betrayed, angry or miserable, be faithful and sincere to yourself and be ready to embrace the answers. Accept all the misunderstood beliefs and start cleaning every dirty spot. You have just started the procedure of catharsis.

Inner fights

This misunderstanding and arrogant behavior applies to the opposite situation as well. Many people after a great victory or achievement stop moving on. They think they have achieved the purpose of their life because it happened to earn more money than they had expected or were promoted or achieved any personal goal. This feat may make them feel great, some may change attitude or become arrogant. They feel they have reached the finishing line and now they are the conquerors of everything and everybody. They stand on their personal pedestal and do not step forwards out of fear of falling down or out of arrogance that nobody else deserves to succeed him. Is this right? Does Earth stop moving on when it reaches a certain point? That would be catastrophic. Do we choose this catastrophe consciously and stop progressing or our big ego makes us feel king of the kings? If I stand on this success, I mire in a wrong belief. We all seek a desire, an emotion, a successful armchair to sit on. Of course, if you stop working, something will remove you from that seat. Humanity evolves and newcomers push you to proceed. If you feel uncomfortable when you have to leave it, it is your problem. You are removed for your own good. Your guardian angel tells you that what you are doing is not the correct course of action. There is no other way to tell you that you misunderstood the law of humanity. If you are hurt, and blaming others is the only tactic that soothes you, it is the right time for introspection. Think about your inner expectations and your hidden intentions. Be sincere with yourself; be open to see your real inner motives, search deep inside you and the answer will emerge out of nowhere.

While you progress and start loving and understanding yourself, a kind of protection is created, to protect you from yourself. If you protect yourself from yourself, nobody can move you. Only if you are insecure with yourself you are unstable. You can see the lives of saints. Nothing moved them because they believed in themselves, because they had worked with themselves. Let's not forget that help does not come to everyone. Only to those who ask for it, because they have worked towards it and have moved on. Ask and you will be given. This is the law of action and reaction. If you don't ask me for ten dollars, why should I give it to you? It's so simple. Everything is so simple.

What is that that makes it difficult? The wall we have built based on our thoughts and convictions and only these are our real obstacles. Every truth is temporary. As you move on you discover new pieces of the puzzle. What it true today, tomorrow it will be partially true because the veil that exists must uncover the one and only truth.

We have to identify the real meaning of a success. If f I discover that what I have managed is not the right thing and led to the wrong result, I must search for the mistake. What did I do wrong? Did I work enough? Was my motive harmless? Was it my real inner motive? Look for it. You have to recognize the mistake in order to find the right result and not repeat the same mistake.

It is like solving a math problem. If the result I found is 24 instead of 32, I made a mistake somewhere on the way. You have to find it. Did you do it quickly? Did you study the theory? Was your thought correct? If your thought is not clear, then the mistaken result is inevitable. Work and harmless clear thought is all you need. You must recognize what is good for you and why you want to look good to others.

If someone tells you that although your result is wrong and you did it well but you just hurried, all he does is pretending to be good to you, he does not help you and he prevents you from finding the right way to solve problems. He just alleviates your hurt ego. We don't need people to kiss our hands and pretend to be good. We need someone to tell us the truth. We must long for people who will show us the right path even though they are full of rocks. We are in desperate need of someone to help us progress and not feed our ego. If we regard these people or these situations as bad, it is again our problem.

The ancient poet Menandros said that a wise man should not repeat the same mistake twice. His words hide a very deep truth. It is important to make a mistake so that you can have the aspect of both sides so as to be able to choose consciously. Otherwise you follow stereotypes, others have set for you. You do what they have told you to do. The basic conscious decision you have to make now you know is to choose the way it soothes your soul. it is not socially accepted for a minister to enjoy skateboarding but it is accepted to enjoy golf. Wonder why he can't do what he really loves. If someone is not truthful to himself, how can he be truthful to others?

The so called bad people are necessary for the evolution of humanity. If you think deeper, you will realize that if Judah was not the bad one of the story, Christ would not have been able to show His greatness and glory. If there was no Crucifixion, there would be no Resurrection. It is the law of action and reaction. It is difficult to understand that the role of the bad one is the role of the one who bears the biggest part of the responsibility. This is an example of looking the internal side of events before we rush to conclusions because this is what we have been told.

So every time you feel out of place, restricted or stressed, open your eyes of your soul to see the collateral beauty. Look for the reason it happened, because nothing happens without a reason. Nothing is told or done at random. Progress means relating facts so as to lead you to the great light of truth, to see the complete picture of your magnitude and not a small part of it.

Facing problems is inevitable. We have analyzed we can't have everything we want. What we have to do is feeling blessed and appreciative for all we have and not cry for what we don't. Difficult moments arise when we are polarized to the bad aspect of a situation. We are blind to see the new state of things. So, having problems is a natural procedure. Our free will lies to finding the way to overcome them. We have to realize that nothing happens without a reason and that's why we must take it for granted but stop nagging and start working.

The solution is not found to being grumpy. The problem does not arise when you learn something and you get hurt. The problem existed but your conscious mind chose not to emerge it. The moment you feel that you are in the worst position it's the time you solve it. Only then you can move forwards and fight. Of course every battle has its losses as well. But let's be realistic. If we avoided injuries nobody would fight in order to be free. Many international heroes lost their lives in order to be able to live free. There is no other way. If they denied fighting we would still live in slavery. And that's exactly the internal lesson of history. To teach you that every time you feel bottled- up you have to fight, even with your own beliefs and see the reason you feel this way. Remember that freedom is the target.

Let's say for example that I found out my husband has had an affair with another woman. I lose the ground under my feet. I feel betrayed and hurt. That's kind of a natural reaction because we have grown up with the belief that this is terrible and it is a pity for the poor woman. Think of it. Every such story you have heart, the same belief applies. The man is immoral, the wife deserves our pity and the other woman is the one that caused this fuss.

We have never thought that this might have been caused because their relation was not strong enough. Being together out of habit never crosses our mind. When I learn that my husband sees another woman, automatically my balance is shaken. Which balance? If there were a steady balance, he would not have felt the need to have an affair with someone else. This is when I start having a problem. At least, this is what others made me believe.

Let's see how many "happy marriages" do not depend on the real pure feeling of love. Many people choose to remain to a marriage because this is the way to feel secure, accepted and my false bubble has been painted pink. If I feel insecure alone, this is my problem and I ought to solve it. If I want to pretend I am happy, this is again my problem. If I am afraid to look at my soul and discover my inner and unique truth, this is again my problem. And guess what? All these "false" problems should be solved by me and only me.

So, when I learn about my husband's affair I feel the earth shaking out of my inability to stand on my own feet. I feel miserable and I am unable to see that this is the moment of the solution. This solution will force me proceed. This solution will move me turn on my light. The problem preexisted, but I chose to close my eyes as I did not want to get out of this routine. Instead of feeling grateful that my eyes can see, I feel hurt and betrayed. My ego has managed to govern me again and I must throw it out once again so as to find my inner balance.

Now, what is this balance? Is it my blindness I had chosen to live in? Suppose a building collapses due to an earthquake measured 3 on the Richter scale. Is the earthquake to blame or the building that had not been built on strong foundations? It is not a coincidence that we use the phrase "build relations". The building fell down with a minor shaking. Who is responsible? The earthquake or my belief that the building was well constructed? What have I done to be persuaded that it was strong? Have I worked towards this awakening? No! That's why the solution is here. Will you feel sad for the collapse of a semi steady building or will you feel blessed you are alive and have the chance to move to a stronger and safer house?

Is the other woman the problem or is she the one that tells you that you stand on crumbling relation? The way you see it, shows how much you have worked with yourself. Your husband's affair is a given fact. Your choice is whether you feel down in the dumps, or thank God you got out of a muddy puddle. That's autonomy. I will feel very hurt if my ego starts driving the vehicle of my soul. This ego makes me start asking how he dared leave me! I am faithful, a good cook, I am beautiful and in good shape! I just can't accept that he abandoned such a shiny star. He must have been crazy! What my ego does not let me see is that he has his own shining star too. And the other woman may shine as well. I am not the only sun in this vast universe. Accepting others' decisions takes me a step upwards. I have to face the truth or I will feel sad because I have to do the shopping alone or I have no one to accompany me in social events. The choice is mine again!

Be the temple of your soul

In order for the soul to grab the power it deserves and make the most of it, get the power which belongs to it, it needs a temple to concentrate all its strength and allies. This temple is you. You are the temple of your body. You should love and respect your existence, take your potential seriously, feel blessed and divine and honor your soul with the worship a temple deserves. Your temple needs believers to listen to the service. Otherwise what's the point of the service? Who are your believers? All your cells are your believers and they are here to obey and follow what you teach them. You have to respect them all, understand their needs and persuade them that you are willing to honor them all. Every single particle of you must have faith they are not mistreated. Faith to whom? To the mystic who administers the mysteries of your life. Who is this mystic? Your own soul! Your soul is your personal mystic who brings you in front of problems. You are the only one in charge of keeping every part of you happy trying to discover the root of these so called problems so that you your believers remain faithful.

Have you ever wondered what happens to you when you take the Communion? What does it offer you? What does it symbolize? How did it change you? Do you commune out of a habit or do realize the change? The essence of communion is to give it to all your believers, from your hair, your liver to your toe nail and unite them. You affirm them that you are always here for them.

You urge them to go on working together. You encourage them to join hands with your soul and cooperate in harmony.

If you don't build your own church consciously, with the power of your intellect, your soul can't be expressed. Your soul is emerged from your mental body. That's the difference between animals and humans. Only humans who have developed their intellect can let their souls be expressed. And your soul becomes your mystic, your hierophant! This hierophant will always show you the right way which leads to your internal light. Your light is patiently waiting for you to turn it on.

When you are able to see clearly the big picture in front of you, you must be happy and not sad because now you are able to see your truth, freedom and love, something you could not have seen in the past. Nor must you prefer your blindness because you were used to it because you were safe with no responsibilities. The point is to start seeing. Those who want you blind, they will try to affect your emotional body. Those who want you trapped giving you small pieces of cheese to keep you happy, will step on your sentimental sensitivity. And they not only present you with false feelings which name them love, but compassion as well. They will do everything to make you feel sorry and lose every sense of the truth. When you can't see the truth which is ahead of you, it means that you are emotionally charged. In our physical field, the higher level we can reach is inspiration. In our emotional field, the higher level we can have access to is enlightenment. Enlightenment opens the door to real love.

Why should someone refuse to see the light? When they first face it they are at a loss. They can't bear brightness. They enter their blindness state again. They prefer the silence of their blindness. They can't imagine that destiny will knock on their door. Be sure to open the door, because if you don't open it, it will break it, destiny will intrude and stand in front of you, taking you off guard.

The problem is if you don't welcome it but try to fix the door. In this case, the same story will go on and on until you learn.

Everything is in the right place, whether you like it or not. You can choose to like it. This is the definition of having a good time. Choose to enjoy what you have to face and try to find the positive aspect of every situation which shakes you. Your cells are faithful to you and you owe to respect and repay them.

Dualities

Our life is full of dualities. Every aspect of our life has two faces. I always wonder whether I shall go or not, whether I eat the cake or not, whether I express my opinion or not, whether I change my job or not, good and bad, man or woman, negative, positive, dark light. This duality defines humans. We are polarized again and see it as a difficulty. Let's see the good side. You have two eyes, two legs, two ears, two kidneys and so on to make your life easier. Don't stand on the negative side. Our creator made us autonomous so that we can make our choices. The energy sent from the universe is polarized passing though great groups of stars. The work needed to be done by us is to break the illusion circle and be able to receive the pure and unalloyed energy of love, faith, wisdom, power. All these are abundant in the universe and our ego blocks them and transforms them in the opposite pole.

What we have to work on and learn is to decide with full consciousness. Whatever your choice is must be made so consciously that you don't care for the second option. Clouds color the sky. Clouds bring rain too. There is no such thing as good or bad. We need both. Every dimension and feature exists to serve its purpose. Everything is in the place it should be. In wisdom hast thou made them all.

Two are the moments of the day that the sky has the most beautiful colors. At dawn when the sun rises and during sunset we can see a feast of colors. The moment our day starts and the moment it finishes. The problem is that we define them as the beginning or the end. Which end do we refer to? Light or darkness? In our duality, we define them as the first and the second. There is no such thing as good and bad! We can say that sunrise is the beginning of the day or sunset is the beginning of the night. We have just learnt to define it based on the light. We cannot understand the work of the night, our subconscious work and that's why we believe it is something negative. Bear in mind that the sun is not lost because we can't see him. The sun goes to its kingdom to prepare the work for the day. So, the sun works when it is invisible to us but this does not mean it does not have a tiring job to do.

With the help of the sun we have already defined the two points of the horizon, east and west. It shows you the most beautiful and colorful way. We must avoid the poles where we polarized, that is the Clashing Rocks, or Symplegades Stones, where according to Greek mythology they clashed together and Odysseus managed to go through. Until you pass through the poles that try to keep you there, you are going to fall from one side to the other and get hurt. Until you learn your lesson, you will name one pole as good and the other as bad. We must also realize that one is the consequence of the other. You can name it action and reaction. The choice is yours again to decide consciously which route you want to follow, the way you want to lead your life. You can choose either from the colorful east to the awe-inspiring west or between the vicious hits of the poles.

The procedure of learning

The big question is how do I learn to take conscious decisions? Let's try to untangle the knots and the twists in order to be aligned with upper happiness and wisdom. First of all, we have to know the stages of the learning procedure.

The first phase is the unconscious ignorance. It is the stage that I don't know that something exists. Let's say, that I do not know that there are bicycles. I have not heard of them before nor have I seen one. So, I am completely ignorant of its existence.

The second phase the conscious ignorance. It is when I have heard of the existence of bicycles and I am aware that I don't know. I know that there are bicycles and I am conscious that I can't ride it.

The third stage is the conscious knowledge. This is when I first try to ride it and in order not to fall I am fully conscious when I ride it. I dare not look on the right or on the left. All my senses are focused on my trial. It is the same stage when a young child tries to write the letters as instructed by the teacher. The kid puts all his effort to imitate the movements that will help him create the letters as shown to him. All his movements are careful and slow because he is not accustomed to it.

The last phase is the unconscious knowledge. It is the stage when I have got used to riding it, I can speed up or slow down as I wish. I can look on the right or even ride it without my hands touching the handles. It is easy to see that when we are accustomed to writing, no one writes the letters as shown to them. Everyone forms them the way they want, the speed that suits them as they actually express their unconscious mind.

After a lot of practice some functions have passed on our unconscious mind which is like a kind of brain automation. You do not think consciously how to ride a bike, or how to write or drink water. This is the reason we must not drive and talk on the mobile at the same time. Driving has been stored in our unconscious mind and talking has occupied all my conscious part. As a result, I am not fully conscious as far as our safety is concerned.

We can also connect this procedure with eating in front of the television. Our conscious mind is on what we watch and our eating is on the automation mode. As a consequence, we are not fully conscious of what we eat, its taste, its quantity and the joy of eating, one of the most precious procedures that keep me alive has been covered by a TV show.

Even if we haven't realized it, the same procedure applies to life. The problem lies to a mistaken belief you have misunderstood. Now you have to go back and solve it. This is the work of dreams. If you work and understand what your dreams have to tell you, you solve it with your full consciousness. The more you delay, the more you are in pain. You will go from one rock to another, from one medicine to another trying to define good and bad. Of course we cannot solve everything but the more you solve the further you progress, the nearer you get to real light.

The great problem we have is not realizing our thoughts or criticism. We are only used to looking at others and not us. Everything we criticize is what we posses. The qualities we don't possess can't be seen on others. To put it simpler, if we criticize or feel hurt of a certain behavior, this automatically means we possess this trait even though we don't understand it. If I am cunning, I can recognize other people's cunning treatment. If we are snobbish we may blame others for being pretentious. This way it is easy to recognize what blocks my forgiveness and sympathy towards others. It has been proved that homonymous repel and opposites attract and this law does not exclude us.

One principle is to pay attention to what people say. We have to be careful to discern if they do what they say. The person you can rely on is the one who does what he says. His words become actions. Most people try to do what they say but they find it difficult because they don't believe in everything they say and they try to do things they don't believe. As you move on, you will realize that what you say will happen. This is a very serious divine procedure; it is the application of the action and reaction law again. If you say things you don't believe or you don't realize the message you send, they will happen and then you will feel that the whole universe is against you without being able to feel the power of your words.

We have to look deeper inside our souls and realize that all our problems come from the past and every stressful situation concerns the future. Where are the precious moments of now? Why do you decide to let your past tie you and feel anxious about your uncertain future instead of living every moment to the full? It is amazing how illogical we can be. Although we have to eat today, we are anxious and lose moments of now worrying about tomorrow. How can you be sure that tomorrow you can have the ability to live? Let our Creator do his job. Have faith that He loves us. We were not born to suffer. Our mind wants us to suffer. We are a product of love. In our natural world it is the love of our parents, in the cosmic world it is the love of our Creator. You are love! Let your cells free to approach and attach to that energy which surrounds you. Open the door of your soul and let your ego go away. It had nothing to offer you apart from misery, bitterness, despair and heartaches

Realization

Do I have the need to find another mum in the face of my friend or partner or colleague? I don't think so. If I have this need, it means that I need conscience to open the doors of my soul, realize that I am a complete universe that can do everything to keep me aligned. It is not an easy procedure but it is a step by step strategy. Every great journey starts with a first step.

And while you want to free yourself from what your parents have put on you, grandparents are a source of sweet memories. You remember events of your grandparents with great nostalgia. You remember them giving you candies, while your parents did not allow you to eat them because they were bad for you. Grandparents are good and wise because they want to correct their own mistakes. They were not like that when they were parents. Now they have the wisdom to put things right. Their aspect of life has softened. They understand that all those years were on the go, on the automatic mode and they somehow can see the vanity of every miserable moment. They do you more favors than you dad who has to work, has responsibilities, has no time to take you to the park, has so many worries and gets angry easily. The way he gets angry easily is because his soul asks things he falsely believes he does not have the time or the right to enjoy. Recalls of grandparents are a sweet hug with the knowledge of life. They know now that they got angry, stressed, felt insecure, and did not enjoy life, for what? For nothing! The great flow or destiny or law, name it as you like, is infallible and unstoppable. If you can't see it, have an inner look and see if your battery has gone low and you have been polarized to the negative pole.

Now, this is your big chance. It is time you crossed all the way to reach the positive pole of your battery. You always have the choice to see a situation as a chance or a problem. Turn your thoughts to the other way and forget that everyone who loses his job must be stressed, everyone who lives alone must feel unlucky, and everyone who gets a divorce must suffer. All these are the beliefs of others, not yours. These beliefs have been passed on your unconscious mind and when you face them you think you are at the bottom. You feel that you have gone down on your knees. Have a look at it the other way round. You must kneel in order to speed up or jump up. It is your choice to raise or continue creeping Study every aspect of life and try to see the inner message. Signs that teach you the right way are evident all around you. So, every time you feel down in the dumps it is the right stance to break your personal record. Every difficulty is here to teach you that you should tune your thoughts to the positive side.

Destiny, predestination, fate, luck

Now let's see what we mean when we believe that our destiny is to blame. At first let's see the difference among the words destiny, predestination, fate, and luck. Destiny is a world maypole and each one of us holds a ribbon. It is the plan for the whole world, but each one of us has a role to play, a ribbon, to hold on to, and move forwards. We are all connected on the top. Whatever is to be done shall be done. It may delay due to the fact that some people refuse to go on, but others will push and surpass them to continue the great plan. Those who delay know that they are not ready to proceed and do what they can to delay others too. Fortunately, this does not last for long to the universe time. It is like a world orchestra that everyone should play its instrument. If you refuse to work and learn how to play yours, it is just your problem. You may well choose to be left out. Humanity can enjoy the concert without you. Your fear of knowing that you haven't worked enough leads you to falsely beliefs that you can delay or stop others as well. It is your unconscious reaction but you are too mistaken. If you refuse to hold your thread, the one who follows will take yours as well. That's destiny, the world maypole that everyone has a share to make it go round.

Fate is your ribbon. The length of the thread that you have access to. Your share. In Greek the word fate is moira which comes from the verb moirazo meaning share. It is your share. It includes all your powers all your talents, all the rehearsals you need to do in order to make full use of them. You may have four or five talents.

How free are you to discover them and offer your little stone to help complete the great plan? Have you discovered them? Have you developed them? Have you walked a bit further so that help others to follow your steps and help them go even further?

Predestination is another word and that means it has a different role to play. Predestination is the part of your share you use. If your fate gave you four talents, how many of them have you developed? If you haven't utilized them, wonder why! Why or what has stopped you from evolving? How strong are you to change your fixed beliefs in order to follow the plan you were born to execute? Have you worked towards it? What has stopped you? Why have you allowed it to happen? If you tell that your parents were responsible, stop it. That happened when you were a kid. They drove you wherever they wanted but this happened when you were a kid. If you are stuck there, it is neither their problem, neither fate's nor society's. It is only yours. Now you are old enough to decide the destination you want to drive to. Complaining and blaming is not the solution. Working and listening to your soul is the solution. Loving yourself is the solution.

Luck is something different. In Greek it comes from the word build. So you built your luck, you destroy it, you kick it away, you make it. It is usually said that someone is lucky or unlucky. This is what he has decided to believe in. Our beliefs and our actions are the ingredients to build our luck. Our choices always have a result. This result is our luck definition; either we name it good or bad. The thing we have to realize is that every decision should be taken fully consciously. Otherwise, we won't be able to decode the results and we say that our fate is to blame. We think we are unlucky and our life is not the one we deserve. This is caused by the fact that we are not conscious of our full strengths and powers. We have not managed to keep hold of the thread and we don't know how long it is, how strong it is, or what color it is. Remember that luck stands on a round rock which is unstable. She is also deaf. She does not listen to you. She is blind too. She does not see whom she gives to and whom she takes from.

Stop blaming your fate or luck or destiny next time you feel you are in disadvantageous place. Think deeper, open your hearts of your soul, stare at it in the core. Have access to your intentions, get rid of false beliefs, fill your inner tank with love and go get your dreams. Nobody is to blame, just our ego that prevents us from working towards our evolution.

Only if we understand what we say, what we do, what direction I want to turn my thoughts to, can we acquire the strength to change all the false ideas that continue to control our mood, our happiness levels, our life. We are taught how to be kind, pleasant and fair to others and nobody ever teaches us how to be kind, pleasant and fair to our self. We respect others, but not us. We do others' favors, but not ours. If we do not respect our every single cell of our body for all the work it does to keep us alive, why should it respect us? If we do not care for our own house, who will? If we do not love ourselves, who will? If we do not feel gratitude for all we are, who will? If we don't help ourselves, who will? I could ask thousands of questions that can make you realize that the only body you belong to and helps you live is yours. However, guilt feelings force you disrespect the most divine entity you were presented with.

The longer it takes you to realize the hidden power of your existence the longer you will feel rejected, hurt, unappreciated, unlucky and so on. If you refuse to turn on the light in your soul, how can you expect others to see how bright you can be? You can be luminous and radiant or dark and dull. Are you willing to work and direct your power of your soul deeply inside you or not? The choice is yours. Will you accept every problem as a new chance or your ego and the fear of getting out of your safety zone will deter you? Will you learn to think positive or will you continue to attract all the misery? Will you thank your Creator for your being alive or do you prefer to be ungrateful? The choice is entirely yours again. Love brings love. Loving yourself will enable you to spread love. Can you imagine if our thoughts, our actions, our beliefs were fueled with love, what a better place our planet would be? One is enough to start. And believe me you are not the first.

If we start thinking in a wider spectrum we will realize how many things we take for granted and refuse to change. We all know the Law of Attraction. A natural law applies to everything, whether it is between the Earth and the Sun or between a pin and a ball. Nobody complains. Neither the Earth nor the Sun. If we disregard it and try to do the opposite, how will we attract the right things? If our actions, our thoughts send negative and miserable messages, how can we expect the positive results to reach us? We live under this law, it has existed for millions of years and do you still have doubts? How egoistic is it to ignore a universal law just because it doesn't suit our misery or takes us out of our comfort.

Step further

If we want to make a step further we need to get rid of our ego. We are good to our friends. Everybody is good to his friends. What about our enemies? Christ is said to be ubiquitous and all pervading. Why can I discern Him in a person I don't like? The grandiosity of our actions defines the magnificence of our soul. Why can't we stand those who have different way of thinking? What have we understood wrong? What is that which makes us mean? If their beliefs are totally opposite to ours, why do they affect us so much as to fill our heart with negativity?

If a friend of mine has made something that hurt me, I should have turned my eyes inside me and see why I feel this way. Did they force me out of my comfort zone? Let's have a more internal look. If they have moved me then I owe them a favor as they helped me proceed. If I were unable to do it consciously, something should move me and since I could not understand it from the bright side, I was forced to realize it through pain. My protector had to reveal it to me. It's my stubbornness and polarized beliefs that I regard it as pain. But that's solely my own, personal, egoistic problem. If I was stuck to a belief, someone should show me there is another aspect as well. If I weren't able to feel the touch on my shoulder, then a kick is necessary to make me look the other way round. Everything happens for a reason and love shows you the reason. Don't be afraid to look at your brightness. It is all yours. Many people out there are waiting for it to illuminate their way too.

In order to proceed, we have said you must undertake your responsibility and the only way to undertake the responsibility is to act consciously. Even the law excludes those who don't have consciousness of their actions from punishment. While Christ was on His cross He said to His Father not to punish the people who crucified Him because they do not know what they are doing. They haven't understood the symbols of His words. He does not ask for their punishment because they are unable to decode His preaches. They just act without being of sound mind. As a result, they are not sinners. This is the first introduction of forgiveness. Our magnificence is shown when we love and respect those who are unable to stand on their own feet, those who have lost their way. So criticizing and accusing someone automatically makes me stand on the negative pole of my battery and as I send out negativity, I attract negativity as it comes back to me. If this isn't the snake eating its tail, what is it then? My wanted grandiosity lessens so much that I keep falling down to the lowest level. It is really sad that forgiveness was taught more than two thousand years ago, and we still haven't understood the real meaning and how it works. The pray Christ left us says: "and forgive us our trespasses, as we forgive those who trespass against us, and lead us not into temptation, but deliver us from evil". If we don't forgive others, how can we expect ourselves to be forgiven? The law of action and reaction is again here in front of our eyes. What's more egoistic than refusing to accept it? Two thousand years later and we cannot even realize what we ask for in our prayers. That's why consciousness is needed. Every aspect of life, everything you do, everything you hear, say the same thing. Be observant and open to the truth. Stop being blinkered. Don't be afraid to face real light as you are light.

We all live on the same planet but not everyone is at the same timeline. That's why you believe that some people are way ahead of others. We recognize it but we do not realize it. To put it simply, it is like someone asking you what time does the sun rise. You can't answer this question as the time that allows you to see the sunlight depends on your position on our planet. It is exactly the same law.

Being able to make our own sunlight become visible depends on the position of our internal evolution. Observing everything and combining information is of crucial importance to enlighten our souls.

The problem is that while we know that undertaking this responsibility is our redemption and try hard to acquire it, when we have it, we don't want it and start blaming our parents or whoever else we think has control over us. This is the problem. We all want to be superior but we do not follow the law of superiority. We refuse to accept the burden of our actions, our beliefs and be holders of our own life. Only when you consciously know exactly who you are can you free yourself.

Another serious realization is that the remorseful sinner is the higher level you can reach. The first person Christ took to Heaven was the penitent sinner on the cross next to Him. What prevents us from realizing our mistake? Hello big ego! Help yourself! Why don't we like being told the truth? Why is it difficult to see another point of view? Why do we have the idea that we are infallible? How difficult is it to understand that the one who brings us to the worst of the situations is our savior? Those who are ready to accept the truth, they move faster and they are able to see the sun going up with all its majesty! Those, whose ego prevents them to see this greatness, they delay and suffer. They have just offered their ego a very comfortable seat.

In order to love yourself, you have to get to know yourself as well as possible. Start working towards the path that leads to your enlightenment. There is no other way to love someone if you don't know him, especially yourself. The more you get to know yourself, the more you love yourself. The more you love yourself the more you love others too and the easier you transform into the energy of love.

At first you proceed and you hit your head because you love others more than yourself. That's natural because others are mirrors of you. You can't realize it at the beginning. You need to look deep inwardly and this work makes you serious. Seriousness is what you radiate due to the work you have done. Whatever your job is, you will end up in the esotericism, the study of your soul from different roads, but we must not forget that all roads lead to Rome.

What we must also grasp is that an idea does not have the same impact on someone. After two thousand years and we have yet to perceive the real concept of love and forgiveness. We see how difficult it is to really love our entity as a whole because we tend to separate ourselves to parts. If I achieve something great, I love my mind, but I don' love my body. If I lose weight, I like my body but feel insecure with my personality. Have you ever thought how all this ideology has come to affect you so much as to prevent you from being happy? If we can't see ourselves as a whole full entity, how can we love us as a whole? Do you see how many mistaken perceptions are on our minds?

It is a very special procedure for an idea to come down on Earth. it is polarized to various energies of the cosmic radiation which is extremely strong. We are saved due to the atmosphere which protects us. What makes it seem different from person to person is the amount of energy a person can endure. It is exactly the same as weightlifting. Not everyone is able to lift the same number of weights. The same applies to the mental concepts as well.

We all talk about the benefits of equality but everyone perceives it in a different way. One may say that equality is good as long as I am the leader. Another may perceive it that equality is good, but I want the leader to love me more than others as I am the best. The third one may think that equality is fine but I must find a way to take the leader's position. The fourth one may talk about the idea of all being equal, as something unimaginative for the first person. As you can see, knowing how polarized energy works makes us more open-minded to understand others. A weightlifter can increase the amount of kilos he can lift by a lot of training and hard work let alone how concentrated he must be. It works exactly under the same rule. We need hard work and concentration in order to be able to lift pure energy and not receive it polarized. In this case no difficult aspect of the planets will affect our mood. Only by being able to become conductors of the energies that reach me, will I be completely liberated!

The instrument everyone has to play in the great world orchestra is part of our personality. What's more, my soul has to be expressed though this instrument. Everyone has his own qualities, let's say one is quick tempered or sensitive, he must make rehearsals in order these qualities to be used by the soul so that the greater plan can be expressed. Everyone should do his best to learn how to play his own instrument without distractions and interventions of egopathic behaviors in order to be able to have a place at the great orchestra when it comes to sing the song of humanity.

Respect our unity

Having expectations is another wrong practice and we continue to count on others in order to feel happy. This mistake can be corrected by a great understanding. Someone who cannot feel happiness for the success of others he may seem ungrateful. Here is another wrongly established belief. Why do I let other's feelings affect me? Why do I allow myself to lower my happiness levels because others do not share my own contentment? Which door have I left open and my ego managed to enter again? Willpower means that I want to do something with all my heart and I don't expect anyone to tell me neither thank you, nor congratulate me on any of my successes. Our willpower is tested by the reaction of others and this is the trap. We let others define our emotions. Why do we let them do it? Do we still need crutches to stand on our feet?

Egoism is hidden everywhere. If I want to help someone and make him happy, I don't buy him flowers, nor do I give him money. This way I try to redeem his smile, or attract him. To be precise, I buy off my good image. I don't offer the help I consider best, but what he really needs to be deceived and look up to me. Do you want to do what pleases you, or do you want to please others? The decision should be taken consciously. Do whatever you want fully aware of your motive and not decide according to what will make others say thank you. This way you only feed your ego in order to become greater.

If I visit a friend I consider it proper to buy him some sweets or a bottle of wine. Without realizing it, I make him feel obliged to me. So, when he visits me he thinks it is proper to bring me something back as well. Who said that? Who defined this belief? Now, if I pay him a visit empty-handed, he automatically thinks that I am mean, stingy, and ungrateful. If I had consciously decided not to fill him with obligation feelings, I am misunderstood. This way I help him get rid of stressful feelings, but social norms force him to blame me and lose energy.

We have seen so many misunderstood emotions which regulate our mood, our actions and by extension our happiness levels which determine the quality of our life. If we get used to all these misconceived perceptions, it becomes an addiction. The more we are in pain the more we ask for it. We get used to this pain-endurance relation and we firmly think this is the right convention to follow. This is not what we ask for, this is not the reason we were born.

Think when we are introduced to a person we have just met. The first thing we inform him of is our profession. Why? The whole of me is not only my studies or my occupation. Is this done because I have nothing else to present of me or do I try to become admirable? There are so many other traits of me which are much more essential than my job but they are of no concern. To put it simply, when we meet someone we have to take notice of his soul and his personality and not his face his money or social status. It is a lever higher on the course of evolution. We have to learn how to unite our physical, emotional and mental body so that our soul can be aligned to the superior energy. Everyone's soul is united to ours. Do you remember the maypole we mentioned above? Everyone's soul is autonomous but they constitute an entity, which has been detached for a while to me, to you, to everyone, but it will unite us all again. It is the great unity that we all exist under its principle.

Has it ever happened to you to meet a person for a first time and feel that you have met him somewhere before, because he looks familiar to you? How do you account for the fact that mums from over the world, not having ever met before, say the same things to their kids and do the same things? Another point that is worth mentioning are the common dreams among people who do not know each other or live on different continents and have a totally different background? To be more precise, we all have dreamt of falling, or going out naked. How can we have common parts with people at the other end of the world? It is easy to understand that something higher than we can perceive unites us. In our unconscious self we talk in the same language.

As we all have parts of the DNA of our ancestors, we all have common parts of the soul of the world. Actually, this is not the only part of humanity we have in common. Our common maypole is the humanity link but let's not ignore that our route is circular and we tend to believe only what we are able to see going on around it. What we hear and generally what our senses are capable of perceiving and understanding are very limited to this cosmic infinity.

When we look to the horizon and we see the ship disappearing from my sight, this doesn't mean it disappears for good. It is still there but my eyes do not have the ability to see it. The same happens with endless situations in our everyday life. We misinterpret the limited capabilities we have of the magnitude of this cosmic entity because our ego and our megalomania do not let us see further. This prevents us from understanding what is there beyond us. For example, we try to meet aliens hoping that they look like us and we believe that they have the same features as we possess. Another selfish belief that stops us from seeing the greater picture has been imposed on our mind. Our eyes are able to see only a certain part of the volume of material called mass. On other planets, life may have another volume of mass which our physiology may not be able to discern. Our paranoid belief is to jump to conclusions and say that we are all alone. Isn't that an egoistic attitude that led us believe we are the ones who have control over life?

The point is to turn our look into our internal part which unites us with others. We pay attention to what others do and not to my whole existence which internally is full of life. We do not bother to stabilize our inner peace and spend time gossiping about others or being affected by what others say. Our skin is a filter and what others see on us. Can you imagine how many millions of invisible mechanisms work nonstop to keep me alive? Why nobody taught me to pay attention to them and thank them and be grateful they do not stop working for my sake? It is time we appreciated the whole of us. Not only what our eyes perceive. My life isn't defined by the color of my hair neither the clothes I wear nor the model of car I own. My life, my body fitness, my mind balance rely on the internal process of my existence and this is something we ought to remember and respect every single day.

Internal symbols

The internal part exists in everything. It has to do with our progress to be able to pinpoint them. The same applies to all sciences. Every science has an internal side but we are not taught of them. What we need to do is work in order to reach this level of understanding. Let's take music for instance. Muses were the ancient Greek goddesses who were considered the source of knowledge embodied in poetry and songs. They are symbolic to the internal aspect of music. What do they do? They take the words to the ether along with music in order not to crystallize them. Have you ever noticed that when you want to remember a song, you sing it? If you just speak the words, you don't remember the lyrics. This is what the Muses do, and particularly Efterpe.

All Greek Mythology is full of symbols. Work is needed to decode them. So is every holy text of every religion. The same applies to every science. When you work towards decoding and start making connections, you will realize that they say the same thing. They hide the same secret. This secret is hidden behind every aspect of our life. Don't wait from others to teach you the real meaning of everything. You have to keep your eyes, ears and soul open to be connected to the higher power, to the ether, to the meaning of our creation in order to be aligned with the one and only entity that we are part of. This secret exists only in our conscious mind acting like a guard who prevents us from conceiving our entity. Actually it averts us from loving ourselves.

Love is the main preach of most religions and it is not accidental. Love is the power that unites us all. If we could get rid of our ego, things would be completely different. The point is that we should all develop our own self-conscience without forgetting that our self-conscience is part and parcel with the conscience of humanity. Self-conscience is important for the function of our whole body and mind. If, for example, we ate junk food today because our nose and mouth were attracted, but my stomach was dissatisfied, we must realize that what sweetens my nose and my mouth may be bad for my stomach. This is how it works. We are deceived by what we can falsely perceive by the external part of every existence as we are not conscious of the processes our stomach follows. Let's not forget that our stomach is a faithful believer of our body who does what we order him to do. If we stop respecting him, it is a matter of time for it to turn its back to his king as he feels betrayed and cheated. We tend to respect everything beyond us and not in us.

The same applies to people. We can be very easily deceived by a nice person with the false belief that his inner part, his soul, is as nice as the suit he is wearing. We tend to imagine that this person has the perfect character, he is the best of friends and after some time we realize that this is not true. This happens because we haven't been taught to look under the "uniform" everything is covered with. It is time we learnt to pay attention to the way we have a nice time, the way our soul is aligned with the purpose we were born and not the way we look.

As we can understand, every aspect of our life has an internal part. As we have already referred to music and the role of the muses, the same applies to history or religious studies. Why do we learn about great historic personalities? Not to do the same things as them, of course. At school we learn the exterior part of a battle, so as to implement the internal aspect when needed in our life. To learn that if you want to win, you have to make a revolution and of course I refer to all facets of live, family, work, friends but first of all yourself. If you overcome the greatest hurdle called ego, then nothing can threaten you.

For the same reason we are taught what Christ or other great religious personalities did. The point is what I can learn from what they did. How I can give birth to God inside me. How I can be the Virgin who gave birth to God. Our minds have been directed to blemish the internal side that will free us. Of course the word virgin is not used in a physical level, nor does it have the meaning of a woman not having a sexual intercourse with a man. The real meaning is that we do not need a sperm in order to give birth to the God that is hidden inside me. There is nothing in common between what we do in our bed and what we do with the divine essence that exists inside us. We all have Him inside us, and we do not need anyone else to manifest Him. He is in us and we must work hard in order to discover Him being born in the cave of our heart.

The word sulfur is synonym to divine and nothing is random in this life. Think of how many uses elements with sulfur have in our body. How useful they are to our health. Combine things; combine all the information you have in order to find the way to freedom. What is the connection of the Virgin to the Virgo in astrology? Of course they are connected as nothing happens at random.

As we have mentioned every science has an internal part and especially sciences that last for thousands of years. They hide parts of ancient wisdom as they carry the knowledge of so many centuries that became knowledge themselves. Now, if we use all this knowledge to see if you are going to win the lottery or when you are going to get married, you smash everything. Everything will be destroyed for a very simple reason. There was no real motive. The only move was your vanity and insecurity for the future.

So much wisdom is not to reveal such minor questions. Our soul needs to be expressed in order to realize our connection with the great higher energy. The energy we are part of, we own and needs to be expressed and not suppressed. If you don't believe that God is inside you, and you are emotionally polarized, you are going to search Him and find Him in every handsome boy or beautiful girl. Then you will realize that He is not Him or Her and start again from the beginning. You are going to blame your destiny or others. Until you learn to look with your internal eyes, you are going to get hurt and be in pain.

Codes of ethics

I am sure that if someone you admire or you want to impress, pays you a visit while you are wearing your pajamas, without a second thoughts, you are going to change and rush to wear better clothes. Why? Why should you choose to feel uncomfortable in order to make a good impression? Why a good impression is formed by the way you look and not the way you feel and act? It is worthy of realizing that while we wear our pajamas we feel happier and more relaxed, but I feel ashamed in front of others. Beware of every action of your daily routine. The message is the same. We give priority to the way we look and ignore completely our inner contentment.

It is time we understood how unfair this is for our soul. We disrespect the whole divinely perfect mechanism that keeps us alive and expect it will never react. Is this possible since the law of action and reaction governs us? Why are we surprised when disease appears? Our internal mechanism has the right to make its revolution and nothing can stop it. It has been our servant before even our first day of birth. It follows our single step, goes along with our decisions, endures the hardships we impose on it, but that's enough. It has the right to tell you that it is not happy, and there is no other way to show it to you apart from illness. Every health problem has its root somewhere deep inside us. If we don't understand it, it is our own problem or to put it better, our own chance to see what we do wrong. It is the time of realization, the time to start loving myself!

The biggest problem we have to face is that we tend to dress, talk, behave according to who the other person is and become liars to our souls. I know many of you would say that it is the code of ethics but I am going to ask who imposed it on us. Nobody told you to disrespect others. Respect others but not more than yourself. If you start believing in yourself, if you really love yourself, you would not tell lies to yourself. We need to be ourselves; otherwise our soul and body will feel like they are opponents. These lies press me and prevent me from being what I really am. Then I expect to be balanced and healthy. Isn't that utopia? What I manage to do is to be kind to my superiors and I squeeze my pressed negative feelings to my interior. This is not how balance is achieved. These ups and downs of my energy are totally destructive. This is where I start losing energy and health problems are a matter of time to show up.

You may think that you are not permitted to talk badly to your boss because you are going to lose your job. I totally agree with you, but think about two parameters you have the tendency to forget. First of all, if you love yourself, if you have collected enough energy, you will have no reason and no need to talk badly to anybody, neither to your superior, nor to exercise your authority to your inferior. If you close your holes to negative feelings, behavior and way of living, then anger finds no place in you. It will not be able to exist in you, because there is no room for it.

Secondly, think deeper and ask yourself who imposed these codes of ethics that direct you how you dress, how you look, how you behave, how you talk. Definitely neither you nor me. People who have the power will do everything to keep it and secure every side of it protected in order not to lose it. They will do everything to maintain their power and will not allow anyone to have it questioned. Nobody wants to lose his throne. This is a social treaty we all blindly accept. We are so influenced by it that it has become a second nature to us. Conscience means realization. Realization means saving you from oppression. Sighs of freedom will help you breath purposefully and the way to love yourself is wide open in front of you.

These codes such as dress code do not permit us to go to the office with truck suits and feel comfortable as it is considered improper. Have you ever wondered why? Do our clothes define how good we are at our work? Are clothes more important than our efficiency? You will never meet a CEO wearing trainers. Does this dress code prove his abilities to run the office smoothly? We have been chosen to be employed by the boss because of our capabilities, knowledge, skills, team spirit and many more, why then our appearance plays such an important role? Our clothes have nothing to do with our soul, our capacities, and our talents. We do the same amount of work even with a suit or a truck suit, but it is forbidden. We should have been judged by our work and not our shoes. How sad to endure to feel uncomfortable with high heels and suffer all day keeping our happiness levels low instead of wearing trainers and have a more relaxed day. This would not affect only our working day, but the rest of our day too because we would not lose energy.

I would like to ask everyone who is in favor of these social conventions, why there has never been a code of practice obliging us to feel free in order to use all our potential. Why keeping employers under rules that have nothing to do with productivity and efficiency still exist? Many will say that the reason is to separate lower and upper class. That's another mistaken belief. Imagine how the most powerful person you know will react if a tap breaks and his house is flooding, or if the garbage men refused to collect the rubbish. What we haven't understood is that everyone is needed. There are not important and trivial jobs. The difference is the income scale and we believe that the only aim in my life is to work all day long in order to keep up with the majority. Stop and think! If we work all day long in order to buy a more expensive suit or car, there is no time to devote to my inner cultivation. Is this what society trends want to pass on us? Ephemeral and short-term riches by crucifying my entity! Is that the meaning of life?

Plato, the great ancient Greek philosopher, in his book "Republic" has given the recipe for a healthy state – man relation based on justice in 375 B.C. He explains exactly how the state and people coexist in harmony. A state free of corruption and injustice and citizens who know exactly their social place are essential ingredients to live in prosperity. Nothing has been done even after more than two thousand and five hundred years later.

Our society with all these codes of ethics separate people by classes and manage to make us respect others by their annual income. If you happen to earn more money, tax advances level and you have the feeling that you belong to the rich. By classifying yourself, you immediately fall into the trap. You separate yourself leaving others behind, just because you pay more taxes and the only thing you achieve is to feed your ego by feeling superior. The problem is that you separate yourself and ignore Christ Who said to devil that the Kingdom is one. In Greek the word devil is "diaolos" meaning "dividing all". Greek words have the ability to express the whole meaning and great philosophers took advantage of them and managed to flourish. The problem is that we ignore all this wealth we have inherited and we have been led to stop thinking, swallowing everything they feed us raw.

We follow trends and practices just to belong somewhere but unfortunately we don't know why. We lack the ability to discover our inner talents just because of the fact that different values are promoted. We praise the appearance and ignore essence. We love our made up face and disrespect our whole kingdom inside us which is what keeps us safe and healthy.

In conclusion, we see that we are affected by others, social norms imposed to us and we forget to respect ourselves. Then, we wonder what kind of life we live and try to find what bothers us, why society is unfair, why our friends betray us. That's because we have forgotten to respect, love and free ourselves.

All our experiences are tools given to us. How will you recognize them? They are those that hard times gave you and you thought they were curses. They are the tools that you do not know how to use them. For example, if on my birthday someone gives me a cutting tool instead of flowers, I think it is useless and feel disappointed. What I have to do is to feel happy I have this tool. I should read the instructions carefully, learn what it does, and when I need it, I am happy to have it. When I was given the gift I felt uncomfortably depressed. This proves that we do not realize the gifts we are given. We cannot appreciate them because we do not know why they are given to us. In essence, difficulties are the tools we are given which we are going to need later. We must not forget that we need to work to find out their operation so as to be ready to use them when they come in handy. Our life is not all roses, but instead of falling into a muddy puddle it is better to learn how to overcome it.

Being faithful to the powers given to us is of crucial importance. What delays us is that we do not act and speak with conscience. We can refer again to the prayer Christ said where we ask for Him to give us our daily bread but we pray without knowing what we ask for. If we have the necessary bread for today why do we believe that tomorrow we will be deprived of it as long as we do our share. We become liars not only to ourselves but even to the God we believe. Because appearance has also been more important than spiritual beauty and awareness! Who do we think we are and believe that we can cheat God by lies? As we can see, a cognitive aspect of our wholeness is essential of freeing ourselves and the way to commence this love relation with ourselves.

Always Remember

Start by paying attention to what you say. Avoid any negative phrase that will return back to you. You know now. Ignorance has disappeared. Find out the wonderful person you keep hiding deep inside you out for fear of being criticized. You are unique and the beauty you were given cannot be seen in your figure but in your soul. Those who love you truly do not care about the shape of your body but the magnitude of your mind and heart. Convert every less into full. Do not feel helpless but helpful, stop feeling hopeless but hopeful. Stop chewing and swallowing what you hear without tasting the flavor of it first. If it is not tasty, spit it out. Do not get overwhelmed by deceitful and misleading problems that others try to load you down. Do not ignore the power of your soul. This is your driving force to evolve. Do not choose to seek light from others. If you discover your own light nobody can manipulate you. Do not stop working towards your personal target. Humanity needs you! Do not let your big ego block your way to enlightenment. You are not superior but you are unique. You are one of the kind and you hold the keys of your preciousness. You are the king of your body, the emperor of your soul. No powerful leader lets others govern their kingdom. Respect every part of you who are faithful to your majesty. Start realizing that you have all the tools needed in order your charisma to be emerged. If you love your entity, you transmit the energy of love to those around you. You play an energetic part to this world and bear in mind that this world needs you. Otherwise you wouldn't have been here. All it requires is believe in you, trust you, respect you and love you.

Circle of life

The circle of our life is divided into 9 stages. Let's analyze these phases and what changes happen throughout our lives. The route we follow looks like the letter U. You have to look at it from high above so just imagine you stand above the gap. Envisage you are the spectator of your life who is sitting above your natural body and watch the journey in this life of yours. Well, as you can see half way you go up and then you have to go exactly the opposite way. We spend half of our lives ascending, and the second half descending. Imagine a pot on fire. When you reach the bottom of the pot is the hardest period of your life because you are closer to fire, you burn and there is no way out. At this point you need to turn downwards and follow the route that leads to self-consciousness. Many people are afraid to change and remain to the hottest point above the fire. They will either learn or burn. Not everybody follows the same timeline because there are delays. These delays are due to your experiences and fixed beliefs that form your personality. We all live in the same place but not in the same time. That's why we say that some people are years ahead, and some are years behind. It is up to the personal evolution and personal experiences of each one of us. Let's take a look at the stages, defining them with age years.

Stage one.

Age 0-18. When we are born, light enters material. Stop and think all the derivative words of material, such as maternity, materiality, maternity, matrix, and mother. They all have the same root as they refer to the same thing. This phase lasts for about eighteen years. It is our struggle to discover and get accustomed to our physical body. Think of how long it takes us to be able to eat alone, to have a bath on our own, tie our shoelaces by ourselves! Some people may remain here for their whole life due to karma or because they did not manage to proceed. Some people's purpose is to just hover here seeking pampering. This phase is when the soul grasps the vibrations of the body, when the soul harmonizes with the physical body in order to coexist mutually and united. It is the first rehearsal in our body and we have to get familiar to it, learn its potential and abilities.

Stage two

Here, at the age of 18-27 our purpose is to get accustomed to our emotional body given to us. We can't see it but we can feel it. At this stage we start wondering whether others like us or not, if they have feelings for us, if we are able to attract others, we make relationships, we experience separation and pain solidifies. This pain is necessary as it is our instructor who teaches us that there are things we do not know. No matter how much we are hurt, we must allow pain to draw out all its healing and therapeutic pieces so that we can find smidgens of our soul. Only then can pain be purified. We need to comprehend that real freedom comes only after pain. It is difficult of course to realize that we broke up with the person we thought we love and be happy to vision that this the way it should be done. It is natural because we have to learn how to jump above all these hurdles in order to stop being afraid of them. Like toddlers. They fall and stand up again and go on until they learn. Likewise, we have to realize that this is the only exit which will lead us to a higher level.

Stage there

The third stage concerns the ages between 27 – 36 years old. The purpose here is to get familiar with our mental body. It is the commencement of wisdom through experience. It comes as a shock to us and we are stunned because we see things that we could not have discerned before. It is the time when our studies, skills, know- how come out on the surface. Something boosts us to express what we want; it is the time to expand our desires, to make changes to our vocational field, changes concerning friendships are unavoidable and of course it is time we expressed our talents. We feel restless and we look forward to a continuous activity. Now, we can understand how superficial our sentiments were and even laugh at the emotions felt back then. Now, our mind is able to judge people and situations by using our intellect and we become better judges of what is happening around us. We have developed skills and knowledge that will help us go on. Without them, our aspect of life was incomplete and we felt pain with no serious reason as we lacked the necessary tools to form our mental body. Now, it is different. We are able to use our critical judgment and avoid falling into muddy puddles.

At this stage, our experiences and knowledge help us become less angry with others as it easier to be in their shoes, we have undergone similar sufferings or joys. Our critical mind is not full of what we have been taught to criticize. We do not get furious with the same things that used to enrage our mums. We are a step further now and we become more tolerant due to our understanding.

Stage four

This stage refers to ages 36-45. This is when our three above mentioned bodies, physical, emotional, and mental get connected. These three bodies constitute our personality. It is called causal or karmic will. It is an important phase of our life because here we reassess and review our past experiences. Here, we come to wonder and try to find out who we are. Reassessment starts. We have full understanding of our physical body, our emotional state, and our mental abilities. All these three bodies are connected and we have to leave them behind in order to go forwards.

We have to start elevating from the bottom of the U. We are close to the bottom of the pot and we have to get ready to make our turning downwards. The great problem here is to endure the fire that makes this pot boil. We are closer to the hottest part of our route. If we stay there for long, we will burn ourselves and if we jump to the other side we get out of our comfort zone. Of course, it is not an easy procedure as passing above a hot boiling part is never easy. What we have to realize is that this is the only way out. It is not to our bad fate but it is the required procedure to advance level.

We don't have to remain to the pain this fire causes but to the purification that takes place. This fire purifies our three perceived bodies backwards. First comes the cleansing of our mental, then our emotional and last but not least our physical body. We yearn to be ourselves but it is not that easy. That's why many illnesses appear at this age. We experience intense fights of discovering who we really are against who others want us to be or who others led us to become.

At this stage it is essential to listen to our souls, our vibrations, our personality, and our real wishes. It is the stage that our soul should be aligned with the syncretism of our three bodies to discover our purpose in life by being able to listen to our inner soul, to let our souls free to remember what our contribution to humanity is. At this phase, our desires and our soul are reborn. It takes power and stamina and the hardest task we have to accomplice is to realize that we have all the strength, resilience, endurance, vitality and talent to do it. There are intense combats, battles and fights we must overcome and come out being the winners. It is time we connected our soul with our personality.

It is important to realize that all this crises phase we are going into, is only to purify our believes perceptions, attitudes that were not even our own but deviated us from our real purpose and led us to believe that social norms and others' wishes expressed us, as well. It is time we followed our soul without allowing social norm to delay us.

As we said before the age standards we mention are only indicative and particularly at this stage some men may reach the age of sixty to get close to this turning.

Stage five

This stage includes ages 45-54. Now we are at the opposite point of the bottom of the pot just after the turning where fire still burns. Purification continues, it is still hot but we head towards the exit. It we understand that this process is necessary, the pain is alleviated. The purpose is worth the pain. Freedom needs fights and struggles with the less casualties possible. It is the time we answered the question "How". How I stand on this world. We feel the need to discover what our place in the great orchestra of humanity is.

This phase is called "divine will". We have been through so much to reach here and now we have to explore what is behind the turning point. We visit areas of our mind that we had forgotten. We had reached the highest top point and now we have just jumped. The choices we have are either to remain still on the top going round and round in vanity with great levels of stubbornness to proceed or feel blessed we have reached the highest point of ascending and decide that the natural law leads us to start descending with wisdom in order to complete our circle in life.

At this point of the burning fire you are afraid to proceed because you want to avoid pain. If you can't understand that you are able for the worse, how will you realize that you deserve the best? We use to say that we appreciate the value of something the moment we lose it. Words are easy, now we have to experience it. At this point we have to use our experience and go on. If we stop here, we will never live what your soul has been incarnated for. We will never discover our real selves. We don't deserve to stand stagnant and scorch just because we refuse to go on. We must not deprive ourselves of the best reward out of fear of this highly hot point.

Our ego has no place here. We must let our souls trust the upper laws and follow the flow of the power we are part of. If we get stubborn and get stuck there, our guardian angel will kick us instead of tapping us to go on. And believe me; this is harder and more violent. It is like you want to wake up someone. First you touch him softly; you tap his shoulder and whisper to him. If he doesn't wake up, you push him harder. If again he doesn't wake up, your pushing becomes more violent. If he insists on sleeping you do everything you can to bring him back to reality. Our angel does the same thing in order we wake up and face reality. If we perceive it as pain, this is our problem and is of no concern to our angel or the cosmic laws we refuse to follow.

This stage is our chance to discover the real pearls hidden inside us. And the formation of pearls is a very insightful example. It is worth combining ourselves to pearls and the reason is well founded. Well, a pearl is formed when an irritant enters a species of oyster or mussel. The pain it feels is unbearable. It really suffers. The fact that we don't listen to their cries doesn't mean it doesn't hurt. As a defense, the mollusk secretes a fluid to coat the irritant so as the pain is alleviated and then killed. It needs many layers of coating, in other words, a lot of work, in order a lustrous pearl to be formed. If we think a bit deeper, we can see that only after pain, a real pearl is created. The same applies to us. We need to experience pain in order to form the pearl inside our soul. The inconceivable tactic is to experience pain and think that this is your destination. No, this isn't our destination, it is our path that will lead us to our real destination which is to free our souls and express our inner power.

The same procedure applies to the diamond formation. Coal in its softest form is graphite and only after going through conditions of pressure can it turn into a diamond. Our decision is whether we choose to remain in the form of graphite or evolve and develop into a diamond. Diamonds have completed their difficult job. Are we ready to undergo all the difficulties and pressure conditions to let the diamond inside us come out and start reflecting light?

Stage Six

This phase concerns ages 54-63. When we manage to jump down stage five and take the biggest turn in our life we need to back out, to stop struggling and rest in the flow of life. This is when we start wondering "Why". Here, we try to answer the biggest question through our wisdom. Our whole life unfolds and we have to understand the route we had chosen to follow. Our wisdom takes over and we seek serenity and peace of our mind. Our desires come first. Time expands and it is the perfect phase to start praying and meditating. We follow the way that leads to our soul so as to be able to add together. Your soul gets calmer. Things start looking simpler and we assess all those things we thought others caused to us only to find out that everything we have been through was the result of our own decisions.

At this phase of our lives we invest in our inner beauty. It is the right time we unearth the beauty we were hiding very deeply in our unconscious mind. Now, we have stopped agonizing for acquiring things, we realize that materialism is not our purpose and real diamonds are those we all possess but have never had the guts to form. Life is calmer and we are able to enjoy experiences we chose to remove their existence from our minds.

We have the time and will to calculate the toll of our actions, beliefs, reactions. We are able to understand why we got hurt, why we chose the way we followed, why all this was necessary in order to get here. It is like being in an underground water well and now we have managed to go up the unstable ladder that leads to light. We see this bright light now and we realize that everything we chose to go through was well worth. The only thing we need at this stage is to realize why we stand at this point. We are able to take big breaths and appreciate our Creator who enabled us to look at the big image with the wisdom we have gathered through the experiences of the previous stages.

Stage Seven

The period between 63 to 72 has to do with our spiritual abilities. We call it "Unconditional love" The most sensitive number is 72. Nagging is commonplace. Nagging is expressed due to sensitivity and the best remedy to overcome it, is to stop judging others and mainly yourself. When we stop blaming others, we get free in a natural way, and this freedom is ready to transform into love. Freedom is love and the only way we love our life. It is the time we appreciated minor things, we are in awe of situations we used to pass unnoticed and show respect to simple matters, we love every aspect of our life and we finally become love. At this stage the remains of our personality come to an end.

When the parts of our personality unite, that is, the connection of our physical, emotional and mental bodies, this stage forms two main kinds of people. On the one hand, they are those who give off light and make humanity brighter, and on the other hand are those who get crystallized. Crystallizing means refusing to change stance of life, they keep saying and doing the same things. Instead of going up the stairs to get out of the dark well to face light, they prefer looking back at the dark hole just because it is what they are used to seeing. This prevents them from moving forwards. They live an endless routine and nagging is unavoidable. We can't feel sorry as it is their decision. Bravery is needed to achieve things and advance level. They have all the prerequisites to admire the breathtaking scenery spreading in front of them. It seems a pity to be only a few steps away of freedom and choose to remain chained. They miss all the beauty they deserve just because they don't believe that their river drove them to the great crystal clear see with golden sandy beaches. Instead of daring to swim like fish and explore every part of this great sea, they remain crabs and try to hide under rocks.

Those who are generous to give their light are happier and freer. They realize that our soul is light and light can't be divided. It is there for everyone to share. It is pure egoism to think that it belongs only to us and we are going to lose it if we share it. No, light is infinite and its healing qualities are endless for everyone to take advantage of. Space is an entity and as everything is in full harmony there, our ego and our short sight make us live in a paranoid vanity.

Open your eyes, your ears, your arms and feel blessed you managed to get here. Your way was not easy and you owe it to your soul to relax and enjoy the presents you deserve. When you sleep, you come back to reality and see where you are only after you open your eyes. When you realize you are safe, your heart smoothes. The same happens at this stage. Open your eyes and try to see that every element necessary to feel serene and peaceful is in front of your eyes. If you resist and keep them closed does not concern others. The choice, and the power is all yours. You have the right to free yourself or keep embracing your ego. You choose!

Stage Eight

Between the ages of 72-81 the type of energy that prevails is "Love, superior Law". We have reached the other end of the open pot, which as we have said looks like the letter U. We tend to recognize spirit in action and we give love a more spiritual dimension. Those people talk without fear. They are not afraid of death because they know now that every one of us is the temple of God and look at themselves through the eyes of infinite wisdom they have acquired through the experiences of the previous stages. The word "old" in

Greek is "geros" which derives from "giras" meaning "prize" People who manage to reach this stage get the prize of life, wisdom and love.

From then on is the open part of the pot. We are able to perceive our connection with the higher energy and we get ready to unite with the superior purpose. We have to appreciate all the energy we have collected. It is not only material things that matter. This is what others tried to teach us. Money is a form of energy. Suppose someone is hungry. We consider we do the right thing when we give him money. But what he needs is food. If we offer him food, that is we cover his real need, we automatically have feelings of remorse and start thinking if we did the right thing, because we haven't given him money. Why is that? Because throughout our life we have been bombarded by messages that money is what can save us, what makes us happy what we must pursue. We were led to believe that our purpose is to make money. If you think this is the purpose of life, you are mistaken. Help has nothing to do with money. Help means covering others' need. We are simply taught that being kind has to do with how much money you offer someone. Would you be happy if you were in a prison and had as much money you asked for and had your favorite food every day? I don't think so! And how vain it is to spend a whole life struggling for a totally false ideal! Our life is not accidental and we should respect it. We have learnt to love money and glory and ignore the real sense of love. Love is energy and the collection of this energy is our power. Our spirit and soul is not fed by money. Why then choose to imprison them in vanity?

We can easily realize that this is not our real purpose. This is not what you actually wanted and your real help involves helping others without remembering what they wanted, they get burnt, suffer and destroy their flow and their health. Nobody gets ill because he lacks some Euros. The problem is never the 50 euro note you do not have. Reality is much deeper than that but the power of money has blurred your inner vision.

Our soul has been trying to show us the way and social trends build a barrier. Now, you have all this wisdom and knowledge you are well aware of the fact that being happy has nothing in common with having money. Now, you can identify all the moments you thought were difficult, were your blessing. Otherwise you couldn't have made it up to this point. Now, you know that every moment is a blessing, every experience is valuable, every person you met was a teacher, and every breath you take is a superior gift.

Well being

It is of crucial importance to realize that our soul drives us to light and love and our personality drives us to the opposite way of vanity causing inner imbalance. The sooner we let our soul express our hidden desires the sooner we will be aligned with our purpose. Think of what makes you happy, how you imagine yourself and work towards this direction. Don't get trapped to what others have and what makes others happy. Talk to yourself, listen to what your inner part has to tell you, and don't be hard on your unconscious part. Try to understand that fighting your soul is a battle that nobody wins. Both your exterior and inner self suffer. Don't choose to lose all your energy looking for something you haven't chosen. You have formed your own personality and you must be faithful to your inner forces. Take a deep breath, relax and imagine what you and only you would fancy doing.

The golden steps for finding the purpose of your life, and manage to live your life to the full are three:

Step One:

The fist and very crucial step is to know what you want. To have a clear target of the result you wish.

It is very important here to speak with your soul, to really realize what is that you want to achieve in your life and consciously know that this result will touch the upper levels of your soul. If it looks unattainable to others, ask yourself why and to whom. If others can't see ahead is none of your problem. If others can't imagine your dream is of no concern to you. Everyone is different and everyone has to offer his different talents in humanity. So, let others dream of their own wishes and chase your own. Imagine spending a whole life chasing others ideals? You will never be good at them, you will never acquire the joy of achieving something, you will feel sorry for all your efforts and finally you will start blaming everyone and everything. That's not fair to you. So, the first step forwards is to know exactly what your soul tells you, to know exactly which way to go.

Step Two:

Being on the alert so as to receive the results of your actions is equally essential and imperative.

This step involves being thoughtful and genius so as to have your eyes open to watch the results you get through your actions. A critical mind which has been freed by sentiments is needed. Christ said He is the salt of Earth. If we decode His words we can easily see that He got rid of the water which symbolizes our emotions and Keeps the essence, the salt. This is the real salt. Not the white powder we use to make our food tastier. Looking always at the internal part of everyday things makes you genius. Another example of this subjected to the natural laws is the qualities of sand. Sand itself is stable, what makes it vulnerable and unstable is water. Water makes sand moving and while it is not stable nobody would ever build a house on a sandy ground. That's why our purpose and dreams should not be based on emotions. Everything tells the same thing and as soon as you realize it, you won't believe in accidental events.

Being able to see if the result of your effort is the one *you* desired saves you time. Don't delay because of your emotional instability. Try and extract the essence. Even if you invested your deep sentiments on this purpose don't hesitate to be critical and see where you are heading for. This is a very important step which is linked to the next one.

Step Three:

The last and equally important step is to be flexible so that if your desired results do not come to the way you imagined, do not hesitate to change course of action.

Many times we do the same things again and again and the desirable result never appears. This is the point where we must change stance. We have to change the way we act and seek our purpose. It is a matter of egoism and sentimental sensitivity that we are stuck to one route and decide to be blind to the other way round. It takes guts to see the truth and realize your mistake. You were taught that you must not do mistakes. Why? If you don't understand your mistake how will you learn? Why are mistakes a bad thing? Who said that? Is there anybody that has never made mistakes? Face them instead of hiding or finding false excuses to support them. A regretful sinner is many levels higher than someone who never followed the way of his soul. Someone who has never tried to be aligned with his inner desires out of fear of being derailed has no important story to tell.

Being flexible to change the way of your journey is enlightening and reviving. It is like going to work following a certain route every day, and if it is blocked by fallen trees you wait there for others to open it, instead of following another route. Don't forget that your achievement is out there waiting for you and only by being flexible will you be able to reach it. Get up and go get it.

The magic words are: Result- Alertness- Flexibility. These three steps apply to every aspect of our lives, from work to well being and to any other dimension, to any achievement, to any plan and every fulfillment. The only thing that requires special care is that the result should be set by you with full conscience. A good idea is to write these words on a piece of paper and place it somewhere evident you can look at every day. Reminders prevent us from losing our purpose.

Our defense system

Let's see the defense system of our body and prove that everything works under the same natural rules. Many people and especially women suffer from cold feet or hands. Have you ever wondered why that is? The most evident explanation is blood circulation. Of course this is not wrong but it is essential that we understand why this is happening and why it affects mostly women in an internal explanation.

Let's take soldiers for example. When they want to protect themselves from a bomb, they are in embryonic poise. It is an automated reaction. They cover their body and face. They automatically take this defense poise to assure that they will not lose their head and main body. The same happens when someone tries to hit you. You automatically put your hands in front of your face and your heart. You don't mind if your hands or your legs are hurt as long as you don't lose your life. It is an unconscious defense posture. We give the order to our brain to shield the parts of the body which if hit, could have fatal results. As a consequence, most of our blood is gathered in the central part of our body and less in our hands and legs. This is a function of our mechanism to fight for our life.

So people who have cold hands and feet, order their brains to be in a defense stance of life and as a result the blood is concentrated in their centre preventing the even circulation in the feet or hands. It is exactly the same whether we talk about a real bomb, or a stress bomb, a fear bomb, a mental bomb and anything that may bombard you. It is a self defense mechanism of our body. The main point is that they are afraid of the attack that approaches them, the attack of life, or the attack of their personal evolution and try to defend their inner essence without realizing it. So, what does your unconscious mind tell you to do? To change position as this poise does not bring you the desired result. Once again we try to cover the problem instead of solving it.

On the other hand, when people are in attack poise, the blood is gathered in their hands and legs because they need the strength to hit, or run. That's why their feet and hands are not cold. These people are ready to fight and react to any situation that may arise. They are on the alert to stand up against any difficulty, change or challenge. They are those who believe in themselves and know that adaptation is welcome while difficulties deserve a real fight.

Our legs are part and parcel of our movement, our body, our mind, our reactions and our stance of life. The messages are sent. The problem is that our conscious part has never bothered to read them. It is a pity that we listen to everybody else and not our inner voice. It is a pity that we are worried for a wrinkle on our skin and not the fight that happens in our nucleus. We have never taken our intradermal self, which is our vital self, seriously and we expect that it will not react.

If we start noticing things that are happening around us and try to connect them with our function, we will realize that our body cries out telling us how it works. If I try to hide the wrinkle around my mouth, instead of discovering why it is there, then nobody else is to blame but you.

It needs work and more specifically hard work. Step by step, connection by connection, after having collected all the parts of the puzzle, the solution will come. The problem arises when you are stuck to the same point and wait to move without making a step forwards. In this case, it is natural to believe that the people around you prevent you from moving leaving no space for you. Nobody stops you from going on. It is your fixed belief that others are better or quicker. Nobody is better than you. Nobody is the same as you, just because everybody is unique. You are unique too. You belong to this world. If you continue to disregard it, you become an accomplice to your soul's, your mentality's and sentimentality's conviction.

Working towards my freedom

We have connected our jobs with being under the commands of our boss, under the strict timetable, deadlines, stress, low salaries, something obligatory that deprives me of my freedom. We regard working as a slavery situation. I hear many people saying that they would like to be rich and have servants at their service. If we try to decode these words we can easily infer that these people feel slaves themselves. And what do they do? Instead of trying to find the root of this wish, they remain in a stagnant position and hope that fate would suddenly make them emperors.

The word emperor in Greek is *autokratoras* meaning the one who keeps himself, the one who has control over himself. Otherwise he couldn't have been an emperor. If he isn't able to recognize what his self tells him, if he can't control his own soul, how can we expect him to listen to his people and have control over a whole empire? Truth is hidden everywhere. Work is what will enable us to see it.

Our assumption and conclusions are that we feel that having to go to my job is a forced curse. We keen nagging every morning, blaming our boss, colleagues, position, clients, everybody and everything we can think of. I am going to ask you and please stop and think before you answer. Suppose a good fairy gave you all the money you need every month, what would you do? Think deeply before you answer.

If your wish is lying in bed all day doing nothing, you are already a loser. This is not a real purpose. You haven't worked internally to realize that we are not here on vacation. The vibrations of your words will be sent and you are not going to like what you will get back. You will be the slave who does not know what to do with his freedom because he asked for it without knowing what the result of he desires is. And don't dare complain. You asked for it.

Always remember the three magic steps: Result- Alertness- Flexibility. As soon as you know the path that leads you to your freedom, cut all the weeds that prevent you from following it, push any rock that blocks your way and start your journey. Success is waiting for you at the other end.

The problem is that we all try to do things with less effort just because we keep hearing that working is tiring and something we should avoid. This belief has entered your subconscious mind and you reproduce negativism without mindfulness. It is like chewing the same gum for ages although you know well that its initial flavor will not come back.

The meaning of the words has been changed and we consider working a synonym of torture, labor and compulsion. This is not true. If people over the centuries did not work we would still live in cages. Would that be a better life? Work means producing, creating, healing, collaborating, assisting, thinking, visualizing, accomplishing, fulfilling, succeeding and many more. All fields are necessary. There are no upper and lower classes when you help humanity progress. All minds and all hands are necessary to evolution. Nobody is here without a reason. The key is to find your reason. And be sure that when you feel happy doing what you can, your soul and body regard you are as their leader and not their enemy.

As we have said, everything has an internal side too. Apart from your real life job you have to work inside too. It is not a compulsory duty you avoid but your freedom path. It needs hard work to distinguish between the result you crave for and the result others have led you to believe it is right for you. Every moment is the right moment to discern if you give time to your life or life to your time. Don't spend a whole life doing things you don't like and when you get old you will probably miss youth. Every moment of your life is precious and it deservers your appreciation. Freedom is at your hands as long as you work with yourself in order to be proud of yourself, respect yourself and reach your desirable result. If you love and feel blessed of every moment you live, of everything you do, you offer and give then universe and the power of love will reward you. The law of action and reaction does not make discriminations.

We owe to be the teachers of our selves. Our souls beg us to set them free. However, if the teacher is somebody else, and this somebody else sets the result for you, then you run nonstop for your whole life and you don't know where you want to go. And then, a moment comes when you realize that you succeed in the targets your boss sets you, the goals society has taught you, the principles you family have advised you on, but your inner desire is something completely different. Inner balance cannot be found this way.

So, let's see how it works. The positive part of wellbeing is the result itself. What is the result I ask for? For example, suppose I ask to have 1000 dollars after three months. This result has already set a problem to my "now". I have to do something so that after three months I have 1000 dollars. How will I succeed in my goal and have this result after three months if I don't move, if I don't work now? And I start to move towards my goal.

The result I set for the future creates a problem to "now". In the same way, every problem I face "now" means it leads to a result to the future. Decide on the result you want and work with great self conscience. This is the meaning of innerness. Our boss, society, parents, friends and anybody else we allow, present us the future and conceal the problem now. That's why you are troubled. They tell you of the money you are going to earn, but they do not tell you of the sacrifices you have to make in order to choose what values more for you. They tell you how nice it is to reach the target they have set for you but they do not tell you what you will be deprived of. All this sounds like cheese in the trap so as to believe that it is your choice. Innerness is exactly the opposite and tells you that your problems now lead to a result.

Beware that the one who must set the problem for you is you and not someone else, because if this is the case, the result will not be good for you, but for the one who led you believe this and maybe for his bank account. Problems are lessons which we must understand that we set to ourselves. If we get hurt, a mistake has been made by us and only us. This way we can change route and correct it. This is a self to self process.

If what you do does not lead you to the result you wish, then change tactic. That's flexibility. The problem you experience today, leads to a result in the future. Beware of what this result is and if you do not like it, you are free to change it. Look at it with your inner eyes and not externally. Let the light illuminate your soul and your true inner self. You must not forget that no pain no gain. Love yourself, love what you do, love the people around you and you will realize that you transform to an agent of love.

Let's see another example. Our target is to go to university and study. This was the way which revealed a new target afterwards. After we graduate, we are still not happy because we can't find the job we imagined nor we earn the money we imagined. Nevertheless, we have already proceeded towards our target. We will realize that this was not only my dad's dream to see me a lawyer, but my heart's too. My purpose is to stand up for the law and defend right. Before we reach our aim we may need to work in a café and serve customers. If you see this as a problem, it is your misunderstanding. Just think that if you did not pass through this path, your ego would be so great that you would not respect anyone. That's why problems are lessons.

If you look at the external part of the situation, and think that serving coffee is wrong and unfair for your efforts to study, do it. Nobody is going to prevent you from feeling unhappy. It's your decision to choose the way you feel. But if you look at it internally, your feelings will be different. In the first case you will feel miserable and blame others while in the second, you will feel contented and free from your big ego.

If your destiny is to study Medicine, whatever you do, whether you like it or not, you will study. Fate will bring you a strict father to force you study, or bribe you every time your grades are high, or deprive you of pocket money if you do not try hard. If it gives you a hard time, the problem is yours. However, if you never had the chance to study and you are a farmer who works hard, exposed to bad weather conditions and hardly gets by, you may blame your parents or your destiny. Again the problem is yours and I am going to explain why. If you look at it from high above and look at humanity as a whole, you will realize that everybody is necessary for the harmonious flow of humanity.

You may have wanted to become a lector and because you couldn't, you became a doctor. At first you may have done it for the money. That's the cheese in the trap again because if they told you that you study to help humanity, you may have asked "why me?" or remember your childhood beliefs and say "others should help me". That's why cheese is there, where cheese may be a good salary, fame, or whatever. Can you see it from above and save people or will you look at the material level and wait for bribes in order to save someone's life? Again the choice is yours, but don't you ever forget that your intention will bring the corresponding results.

You have to understand it sooner or later that whether a doctor, lawyer, farmer, chef or barber you are useful and helpful to humanity. The sooner you understand it, the higher level you reach in consciousness. You have to realize that along the way you are going to meet a demanding boss or hardships. Neither the boss nor your hardships are the problem. They are just on your way. The problem will be solved when you realize that the only one who gives orders is you. Along the way, many people will take advantage of you, cheat you, help you, just to give you a boost to find yourself and realized that it was you who allowed everything to happen. Bear in mind that experience is much stronger than emotion. When you accept the law, you will be free to love yourself and others unconditionally.

Getting older

Many times, we do not bother seeing why things are happening to us and trust others. This happens in the world of the cosmetics too. Instead of trying to see why that wrinkle appeared, we are in a state of shock and try to hide it. It is the easy solution when you are not willing to work. You just go to a drug store and buy a cream. The bad thing is not to buy a cream, but to refuse to work towards the cause of the wrinkle. We have to realize that our body is the cleverest mechanism and the only thing it asks us desperately, what it only needs from us is to understand it. We have to understand that our body has everything we need to be healthy as long as we understand how it works and activate the mechanism to achieve health and happiness. We are not designed to get ill or get old so quickly. This is happening because we do not listen to our body. And the irony is that only our body, in all its aspects, is really ours.

We learnt to respect others and not us, we are used to be kind with others and not us, we value others and not us, we respect others more than us, we love others more than us. That's enough. Everybody is responsible for himself. This love has nothing to do with selfishness. No, exactly the opposite happens. If we give ourselves what we deserve and gather all the energy of love we need then we can give it lavishly to everybody. I am going to say it again and again. If I do not have any, what am I going to give others?

Many people experience a shock when the signs of ageing knock on our door. We are not prepared to face them and that's natural because we never tried, and never took our body mechanism seriously. We never listened to the messages it constantly sent us. We took it for granted and thought that we are the masters and we can conquer and regulate our body. Our vanity in its all magnitude is evident.

When we face this kind of despair we continue to be lazy and refuse to discover our body and turn to the easiest solution. Wrinkle? The answer is the best cream according to my budget. As you can understand we continue to ignore the messages our body sends us. This message may be any pain, any change, any worry, any spot, anything that will make me feel uncomfortable. There are two kinds of reaction. One reaction, the internal one, is to see why this is happening and the second, the external one, is to think about what I can do to cover it. All reactions of ours have two faces and we are responsible to decide which one leads us to our freedom.

It is very important to realize that our body has everything it needs. Our body is a perfectly oiled machine as long as our tank is full of love and resilience. The problems start when we run out of this revitalizing fuel, love. Let's take the example of face creams. Our face does not wait for creams to be moisturized and fresh. Our organism produces its own moisturizing cream. Our organism needs air and water. We are earth and fire is in us. Oxygen is transferred through blood and water revitalizes and moistures our body. Why do we need a moisture cream then? Why don't we wonder why these functions of my body stopped working efficiently? Why baby skins are so tender? I am going to remind you the great difference between adults and kids. Kids live for their every moment, they never worry about what they are going to eat the next day, express their thoughts automatically and they tend to forgive instantly.

Adults are full of responsibilities. What we haven't solved in our minds is that undertaking responsibilities does not mean loss of energy. We have misinterpreted the sources of happiness. That's why adults have wrinkles. Somewhere between childhood and adulthood there has been a mistake. Have we stopped to appreciate every single moment we live? Have we forgotten how it is to forgive or have we stopped expressing ourselves? The worst aspect is to forget that we are the kings of our body. We are responsible for every action of my mechanism. If I disrespect my empire, then I have no right to complain if they dethrone me.

Now, let's see what we need for a good cream. Squalene is the best nutrient for our skin. It can be found in shark livers, olive oil and a plant called helichrysum (chryso means gold in Greek) It replaces the natural fat of our skin. Why fat? Because birds of a feather flock together. It is a kind of homeopathy. So, it restores skin fat with fat. We also need beeswax. Our skin produces it but it disappears by ageing. Now it is replaced by hyaluronic acid which is a substance that can keep six thousand times its weight in water. That is, one gram of hyaluronic acid can keep six kilos of water and it is kept swollen hiding wrinkles. Our body has everything and I do not need any extra substance. Unfortunately, our natural sources reduce and disappear by aging. Here comes the point to ask your inner self! Do you want to find out why they are dying out or don't you accept the fact that they ebb away and try to maintain them?

If we want to see why they ebb away you have to understand that you must pay attention to your inner self and not outside appearance. It is better to have a bright skin because I have a bright soul. It is more important for my eyes to be able to radiate than their color. If I cannot do that, then I try to replace all the pieces of my inner self which are lost. Now you are going to ask, how can that happen? It is so simple as to give that order to my brain even though you cannot understand how it works. Do you really have consciousness of everything that happens in you? Can you find the unconscious way that the food you eat is transformed into nails or hairs? It all needs work. You can give the order to your body to transfer oxygen to your face and restore all the wax.

There two ways, internally or externally. Both of them can do the work. The choice is ours. If we choose to cooperate with my inner self and try to find out what the wrinkle has to tell us, we apply the rule of flexibility we mentioned above. This way we are ready to realize that this is not the only way to attract others, but we have to understand that I must radiate the beauty, gold, and light I have in me in order to attract others. Every coin has two faces. Both of the choices are possible as long as you choose one consciously.

If we try to express this in a different way is either trust yourself or others. The dilemma has to be transformed into a lesson. If I trust myself the benefit returns to me. If I trust others the profit is theirs. Look at the signs the body sends you in order to listen to what it strives to tell you. It just wants you to be satisfied, happy and healthy. It does not need your money; it does not want to sell you anything.

We talked about ageing and let's approach another aspect of it. We are stuck to the things we were able to do in the past, either you call them responsibilities, the pleasure of helping others, or gratification of being useful. It becomes a habit and we forget that moderation in all things is the best policy. Our strength is not the same as years go by. Others should learn to help themselves and not take us for granted. We have gained the experiences we meant to have, we fulfilled our purpose, but if we respect our body we must start freeing ourselves from unnecessary pressure and anxiety.

That's the reason we have to distribute our burdens and stop pulling other's weight. It's time others learnt how to do the work themselves. When you do not share or distribute the burdens, pain sneaks into you and it is a matter of time to manifest itself and experience it. Nobody wants you to be in pain. You haven't set the limit and thought your inner part would never react just because it tolerated you for so long

If you consider others are not able to manage the new situation, they will definitely believe that they are incapable of doing what is simple for you and they don't even try. This way, you don't help them because you don't give them the chance to prove they can manage equally well with you or even better. They are deprived of the chance of learning to work. If they learn that working is freedom you will become good and even better that you.

Is that what you are afraid of? Not being high on the chart? Can't you stand the fact others will stop thanking you? That's egoism. It is this dipole that knocks on your door again. Your ego does not let you accept that others are also skilled fighters against your inner mechanism. You strain your body and your persistence to act this way will cause the respective reaction. Then, try to find out why your nerves are a bundle or your back aches. Both you and others lose but you are the one who suffers.

Remember! Our creator did not bring us here to suffer. How ironic though it is. We, ourselves choose to suffer. Why? Does this make us feel important? Do I complain of having so much to do because I beg for others to feel sorry for me? What power drives me to seek the mercy of others? Has this become my routine which keeps me busy all day out of fear of being friends with myself? This is another realization we should take seriously. Negativity prevails along with our blessings. It is so evident that this method leads to the wrong result and we still continue to embrace it.

Even when we are with a friend and starts telling a problem he faces, our mind automatically tries to find a worse situation we have been through. No! Loving myself means I don't have the need for others to sympathize with me nor feeling mercy for me. No, that's enough. It is time we changed and loved ourselves. Loving myself means being filled with love and being able to share it lavishly. Loving myself means I am full of light and I can light others' path too.

We can feel important, useful and necessary only if we get rid of any egoism which blocks our flow. Loving myself means collecting love and brighten my path so that others can follow and continue to open pathways after me. But I must trust them. I must know that the earth and the universe do not revolve around me. I am one of the many, and although we do things different, although we look different, we speak a different language our aim is common. We all have a share of the same maypole. We all deserve a ribbon. Helping humanity is not a one man's job. Everybody is useful and welcome to put his little stone in order to build the great kingdom of humanity where love is abundant and undistracted by opposite powers.

Hardships are the part that makes you stronger, but until you realize it you just feel pain and think that somebody punishes you. No, nobody wants your punishment. What is needed is to understand that through every difficult situation you come out stronger.

Films are a great example and especially the American movies which are pioneering and with greater success in comparison to others. Why? Because of the happy-end they introduced. They show us that every change is for a better result. In most scripts something bad happens to the main hero that takes him out of his happy daily routine. He loses something whether it is his job, his wife, whatever. After struggling with all his power, he manages to overcome any problems and finally he is in a better position than before. He does not realize it through his journey and sees only obstacles in front of him but he ends up being in a much better condition more conscious and appreciative for what he has. As you can see we can also learn many important lessons from movies.

The same happens to us. Every change is the only way to allow something better to enter even if you do not understand it. And what a pity people are afraid of changes. They prefer staying stagnant in a situation they do not like just because they are afraid to move and they do not want to work for better results. And they continue to suffer and blame their destiny.

Have you ever wondered that if I do not enjoy my life, if I do not follow my heart, if I don't listen to my soul, if I turn my back to my happiness just because it is not another's happiness, when will I have a nice time? When do I expect to rejoice? Unfortunately we believe that the only motive to work is money. The point is to avoid getting caught in this net. What is the meaning of money if I die rich and have left happy moments surpass me?

Last but not least, choose to be on the side of those sending positive messages to the universe so as it returns back on earth and by extension you. Don't choose to attract negative energies which delay humanity to evolve. Don't pay attention to what others say before you have listened to your heart carefully and affectionately. Remember not to be affected by how others react but work towards the way you react and find out why some situations have moved you. Don't think that doing nothing is a blessing, think of the possibility planets or your body stops moving. Distraction and inactivity are not your desired purpose. Feel blessed and make most of your voltage and potential. Show the world that you are not an observer here but an active member who does your best to contribute to the collection of cosmic love so as to reform the aura of this world. Make sure your mind keeps pace with your soul. Being aligned brings harmony and love is free to unfold all its magical qualities in order to bring an end to fake and deceitful suffering we all experience personally and collectively.

Dreams

In order to love myself it is of crucial importance to know how my inner mechanism works and try to decode it. Dreams are not incidental and that's why I believe it is worth including in this book. Dreaming is a huge topic to cover as it includes all the secrets we struggle to find out during our lives. The problem lies when we try to explain them as it suits us or according to what we have heard. The only one who is able to explain what the secret messages tell us is the person having the dream. All others act like helpers. Of course there are common parts that everybody steps on. As we have said changes happen for a very particular reason. If we receive them as good or bad depends on our own level of advancement. At first, we are seduced by our own experience and practice mirror thinking. We forget that if we are ruled by our personal emotion we must be ready to receive our own arrows and be betrayed from within. It is very natural to judge others or situations this way but are ready to receive the familiar arrows back?

Likewise in dreams, we tend to interpret them as it suits us or we avoid giving explanations because we are afraid the eminent change. For this reason many people stop remembering their dreams. Actually, they turn a blind eye to what is going to come. Don't forget that change is going to come whether you like it or not. Your choice is to decide if you want to be prepared and face it or let it surprise you. Realizing that whatever is happening serves a particular reason is right sense and correct judgment. If we can't see the collateral beauty and regard them as bad fate has to do only with our own poles.

Dreams hide the secret of our future. What dreams try to do is to solve our problems, show us solutions so at to get to know ourselves. This can be done by concealing desires, revealing past events, or cheer us up. Whatever energy we receive, in essence, is our helper. They help us discover who we really are. Dreams will use any language they can so that we can get the message. Every language uses its own symbols, like mathematics, English, Greek, Chinese language. Dreams use symbols to tell us what is coming.

If for example I had an argument with a colleague of mine, my dream is going to show me what my unconscious mind has to tell me. It will give me the answer if worrying was the right thing for me to do or I shouldn't have got upset. Of course this message from our unconscious mind is in conflict with our conscious part.

There are some very interesting theories and approaches to dreams. One theory defines dreams as our desire fulfillment. It is exactly the same as the old saying that the hungry dream of bread. Another one states that we have dreams in order to adopt the analogous disposition the day after. For example a pleasant dream will affect your mood pleasantly but a distasteful dream will affect you negatively. A third one explains that we dream of past flashes, that is, parts of our archaic past.

Other theories state that our dreams are affected by how we felt before going to bed or they are associated to a heavy dinner. Our blood circulation of our brain is totally different when we go to bed with an empty from a full stomach. An exterior situation can also affect our dreams. Suppose a young girl has high fever and dreams of being in a place full of fires. This is because she has been taught that bad people go to hell. If she believes that some time in her life she did something unacceptable by her mum and feels remorse fever will be connected with hell. If her conscious mind is clean from guilt, she would more probably dream of sunbathing.

Every dream contains a part of moral issues. We dream not to solve the problem of high temperature but her fake belief that she is immoral. Think of someone who is a faithful husband, a perfect father, is a very respectful businessman and his image in society is that of the ideal man. If all this is done just because he has been taught that a decent image is the highest virtue but he would like to sleep with another woman, what do you think he will dream of? Of course other women! His unconscious mind tells him either to go and stop suffering, or stop thinking of other women so as his soul stops suffering.

Another theory is that of our personal memories. If for example my mum humiliated me when I was a child and felt so badly that I hated her then, I may have a dream that burglars hit her. My conscious mind does not allow me to do it myself because of course I don't want my mum to get hurt. It just reveals past personal memories. This kind of dreams is quite common to children.

Another theory I am going to mention is that of premonition. Many people believe that their dreams have a sense of a prophecy. These prophetic dreams are not for everyone. First of all you have to gather so much light so as to be able to give others. Have you worked hard enough so as to be able to help others? Why then future should be revealed to you? Dreams contain prophetic parts when you can do something for others. Otherwise we interpret them this way out of fear.

Let's give an example. If you dream that you suffer from cancer, is this prophecy or not? It may be but a lot of data need to be acquired in order to answer that. If you undergo the necessary examinations, you will find out if it is prophecy. Logic says that the your first thought is not prophecy because you have done nothing to advance your level. The most probable reason you dreamt of that is out of fear not to suffer from this disease. Your unconscious mind tries to tell you stop thinking negatively. You must turn your thoughts into your positive pole otherwise you won't like the result. Your dream tries to save you from bad consequences you attract by being pessimistic and fearful. Then you may wonder if you have cancer or it is you that causes it?

Indians used to believe a lot in dreams. They thought that if you dreamt that you stole something you are a thief. Doing it or not is of little importance because only ethical boundaries keep you from doing it.

Dreams set two different powers free. We tend to call the power we approve of as good and the forbidden force as bad. We shouldn't bother to find out what is good and what is bad but unite these two powers. Our purpose is the unity of opposite ends in order to become one kingdom. Our kingdom. If I oppress one of these powers, our subconscious part will try to communicate it to me before a revolution happens inside me.

Plato said what exceptional men act while they are asleep others do it while they are awake. He means that I am an exceptional personality when I am able to beat my urges. It is such a wise aspect because if my thoughts are balanced and my soul is free, I have nothing to fear of. In other words, if I have no need to steal, do harm to others, or suffer including any other negative thought, I am going to dream of something else and not my oppressed desires. In other words we dream the opposite things from what we do.

Solution comes when we heal our mental level and there are no opposite powers in me. It is very important that we let our conscious part approach and welcome our unconscious part so as unity is achieved. This leads us to discover who we really are and find out every wish we have suppressed. Our DNA transfers knowledge from the very ancient past and that makes evolution because if we manage to heal these parts, our descendants will stop suffering from them. It is our duty to save humanity and unite these antithetical and diverse powers which have control over us.

It is like dark fights against light. Say it as you like. Bad against good, males against females, ugliness or beauty, poor and rich, it is the same thing. They are all dipoles. If we stop fighting against them and fully understand that they are both ours, then we will be able to have full conscience of what we are. Only if we manage to marry these antagonistic impulses, will next generation feel free and undistracted to thrive.

Acquiring conscience means understanding how dreams work. We all ask for solutions to our problems and because we can't solve them we go to bed. Solution does not precede sleep. You think that this way you will relax and forget it, but you forget that the purpose is to solve them. The point is not how to take revenge on those who hurt me. In this case it means that you haven't understood something. Something is missing and these negative feelings have overwhelmed you. Your dream is going to explain what you have misunderstood. Sometimes our big ego refuses to accept them. Never forget that dreams are going to lead you and help you proceed.

Our mind is full of moral rules and restraints that we expect our unconscious part to express our inner thoughts because our conscious part dares not talk as it always seeks the easy way. It feels safe this way. That's why dreams come, to move us and show us the solution. In this essence our dream is a more sincere part of us than our behavior when we are awake.

We don't dream for fun. This invaluable function is going to lead us to evolution. Our society has achieved so many advancements and yet to discover ourselves. It seems a pity that we can't understand the functions of our mechanisms and we continue to resist accepting their importance. Dreams project a new situation and we are afraid of this change. We are stuck to old beliefs and refuse to accept the new one. Who told you that the new situation is going to be worse? This is your negative pole talking again and has nothing to do with cosmic evolution. The trap we fall into is thinking that every new situation is going to make us feel uncomfortable and we stop proceeding. If we stop, everybody behind us stops too and then we complain why progress does not come.

It is worth noting that dreams have only to do with the person dreaming it. That is, if you dream that I have died, it doesn't mean I am going to die. Who are you, and how much have you worked internally so that what is going to happen to me is revealed to you? You don't actually dream of me, but what you see is my star print. What I mean is that you actually identify yourself with some qualities of mine. Let's say for example that you consider me as a very dynamic person. Your dream actually tries to tell you that your dynamism is dying, not me. You have no power over me. Get up and go find yours first.

Suppose we all see the same person and when we describe him, one will tell he is tall, another sturdy, a third one will find him pleasant, someone else may notice his hooked nose or his big feet. We all describe the same person. Only upon unity can we possess the whole of everything. The same applies to our conscious and unconscious mind.

The truth in dreams is not the truth we are used to. It is like the truth in poetry. Poems are not fully understood as novels. Poems and dreams touch your soul and not your logical part. Dreams use symbols which are not the evident ones. They hide their meaning internally and their codes are not easy to be decoded. It is when someone tries to hide his feelings by revealing them. Imagine someone tells you that he finds you very attractive. You want to hide your embarrassment and you flash. Do you conceal or reveal your feeling? Actually, you are trying to hide your emotions by revealing them. You flash in order to avoid showing our feeling and by flashing, they become evident.

Dreams express our unconscious mind and walls erect as long as I build them. Every day experiences affect dreams and you may dream that you are working. No matter which theory you use to interpret them, the dreamer is the one who can decode it. Your unconscious mind will not tell you if you work or not. It is none of its business. We all know what we have been taught, that is, that we all have to work, so being unemployed will make you feel sad. Your dream tells you that whether you work or not, do it with full conscience. If you decide to work, stop complaining that you get tired, you have no time to go out and so on. If you decide not to work you have no right to complain that you don't have a lot of money, or you can't buy a new car. Your unconscious mind tells you that whatever you do you must perfectly and wholly unite your conscious and unconscious mind. Whatever you choose to do you must do it with full conscience. The purpose is to unite these two parts of our brain and dreams try to do it by using symbols, and these symbols bring the unity of these parts.

Only in unity can we fell relaxed, happy, satisfied, serene and blessed. Consequences are unavoidable whether you do things unconsciously or not. What we have to understand is that we must enjoy every moment. We must not think how nice it was back then, but how nice it is now. Not a single sign or moment is random. The problem is that we don't understand it and that's why dreams come. We must make associations in order to see the truth. We should not care about what we do in our sleep but what you don't do when we are awake. It is easier to do things in our dreams than in real life. Difficulties arise when we are awake. (In Greek the word clever is exypnos meaning coming from sleep). Ingenuity means combining things, events, and signs and tries to connect them as long as we remain to every new "now" and don't get polarized to past events.

Structure of dreams

Every dream as every one of our actions has three stages. The same applies to words and we are going to analyze these common phases so as to understand what we dream, what we do and what we say. These stages are also very important to recognize others actions and intentions so that we are not affected by our sentiments and lose reality.

1. The presentation of the problem
2. Trial to process the problem
3. The solution

Let's analyze these three phases and make some connections. At first, your problem will come up whether you like it or not, whether you realize it or not. Your subconscious mind just shows you the situation you are in, what you have in mind. If we connect them with our actions is the thought of doing something. For example you realize the reason you want to go to the kitchen and have a glass of water. This is your intention. We don't always want to fill a glass of water because we are thirsty. I may want to throw it at someone's face. I may need to drink so much water in order to fill my cyst for an ultrasound examination. The same part in a word is the preposition, the first part of a word. It is important to note that in Greek the word preposition means intention.

The second stage is your trial to act and do whatever possible in order to get out of this situation because you feel unconfortable. In dreams, it is the part that you fight or act. It is the part of the dream you find awkward and difficult to understand. If you are not ready to see the end, you wake up at this point. When you wake up you feel relieved or at a loss. You can't understand how you got involved in this situation and many times you wonder what you have to do with all this. From another aspect is your action. It is when we act after thinking of something. In grammar, this part is the main root, the verb of a word. It is not random that in Greek the word verb or act is also called energy. It is the energy I need in order to act.

This part of dream is the largest and the most common one. I need energy to go to the kitchen and fill a glass of water. The problem here is that now I have to throw it on your face or drink so much that my stomach is full. You believe that there is no room for another glass but you have to drink it. There is always the possibility that you went to the kitchen just to leave the tap running so that I have to pay more because you want to take revenge on me or feel jealous of my having more money than you but you feel anxious in case I find out. Here you have to face the conflict between your mind and soul. The problem arises when you are not fully conscious of your action and you were not sure of your intention, your preposition.

The third stage includes the solution. It is the outcome of your action. In Greek language the word suffix is synonym to solution and outcome and it hides a huge truth. It is the part of the dream many people do not stand to face. It is the result and you wake up before the solution is in front of your closed eyes. It is the part of your action where you throw the glass the water on my face and now I am so angry that I start shouting at you. You can't stand it. You want to avoid this last part and that's why you wake up. It is the revealing of your real character and you have no excuse because you realize your fault. Many people can't stand their faults and try to hide them in order not to crease their falsely spotless image. Now, I have understood who you are. The real problem is not me but you. Are you ready to take on the consequences of your action?

Will your action bring you to a stronger or weaker position? This has to do with your intention. As words, like actions, start from the proposition- intention, be careful of want you intent.

Our dreams like our many other aspects of our life include trinities. Whether we call it presentation – process – solution, or preposition (intention) – action – suffix (result). In scripts we call them set-up – conflict- resolution. The great Greek philosopher Aristotle called it Beginning – Middle – End. All of them are true and they say the same thing. This is the trinity I have to tame and be conscious of and unite it.

It is common as we have said to wake up before the solution because you can't endure the end. That's why dreams that wake you up are important. They present you the problem and if the process, your action is not successful, you wake up out of feeling tired.

When you are awake and you feel tired you go to bed. When you are asleep you also wake up out of fatigue. Dreams add problemς so as to move you go on. There is no other way to communicate with your unconscious part and free your selves. You try to hide problems that take you out of your comfort zone and you falsely believe you are balanced. When you wake up you believe that you escape from this uncomfortable situation but in essence you avoid feeling it. That doesn't mean it neglects you, though.

Many people tell me that they have the same dream over and over again. This is the stage of presentation. You dare not even go to the process phase. If your dreams are discouraging, this means that your thoughts have stuck to the problem itself. You may call these dreams a nightmare, this is of no concern to your subconscious mind, but they tell you that you have been cemented to the problem and you have doubled locked the doors for the solution to come. It needs work to move on to get from the sofa we have been sitting comfortably and open the door.

Our subconscious part of our brain hides secrets and problems you can't recall where they stem from until we face them, without fear and let them come out. Welcome a very difficult situation you are trying to bury. Unfortunately they do not discompose and they do not disappear. Treat them with love and care. They come back to remind you that your word has the suffix missing. Your word is deficient, but your purpose is to be whole and complete.

Only when you solve the problem you will not allow disease to affect you. You get ill when you refuse to change and the disease itself shows the way to healing. As we have said every problem concerns one of our bodies, physical, sentimental and mental. Solution waits to the upper body of its manifestation. What we need to do is identify the root of the problem and work towards the advancement to an upper level.

We have to understand that we can't hide from our real whole self. Our subconscious mind is always present regardless of the fact we can't realize it. It is in you whether you are awake or asleep, while you are driving or cooking. It finds some moments and comes out. It is easier to identify these moments when other people are talking. Their unconscious mind always shouts. The same happens to us but our sentiments do not allow us to recognize these moments. If you start being more observant you will realize that it emerges without us being able to control it. And it always tells the truth you wish to hide.

Between our conscious and unconscious part, there is a guardian that controls what information is allowed to pass the gate. He stops every piece of information is not allowed to come out to our conscious part. That's why messages are transformed into images of beloved and accepted things or people, hiding all the wisdom and knowledge which we are not aware of. There is no other way to cheat the guardian pass this door and emerge. The work we have to do is connect to the maximum extent these two parts.

Symbols

Trying to find the message dreams tell you is not a simple thing and it differs from person to person. Everyone has the cosmic knowledge, which is our DNA, but there are many other necessary factors to be taken into account. Personal evolution, beliefs, experiences, social background, age, mental functions, personality, temperament and many more constitute our mind library. We are all different but there are common beliefs among us. Let's see some symbols our brain uses to show us what it has to tell us.

Falling- flying

Many people dream of falling or flying. According to theories there are different explanations but let's see a simple one. Can you remember when you were young and your dad used to lift you in the air and then catch you? Of course not, because you can't recall memories from back then. Your brain library though, possesses these memories. Start observing what happens to a child's face when his dad throws him and catches him. The child feels so ecstatic when he flies free and at the same time he feels so secure that his father will catch him again in his arms that the child really enjoys it. The hidden message is that we must feel safe that our Father won't let us fall down ensuring us that we are safe. In another situation it may hide a sexual desire, or it may be just a memory of monkeys falling down trees. It all depends on your experiences and what you go through at this period of your life.

Naked

Many people have dreams of going out naked or without trousers or shoes and you are ashamed that you are not properly dressed. If you are able to remember some details of your dream you will realize that nobody cares about you apart from you. The only person who feels awkward is you and nobody else cares about your body or your clothes. The hidden message here tells you to stop feeling that you must always be perfect. Others do not care about the external part of you, but your inner part is what it counts to them. This fixed belief also shows that you judge others by their appearance too. Your dream tells you that others accept you as you are and not according the clothes you wear. To be frank, nobody else cares about what makes you feel uncomfortable apart from you. If you think deeper about it, it will save you fron unnecessary stress.

House

Rooms symbolize the parts of your body, while a cottage may symbolize calmness, relaxation or even our purpose. You see that we must make logical connections in order to find the hidden information. Don't forget that dreams use symbols that our conscious mind regards them as acceptable. If you see a building falling, it tries to tell you to throw off your ego.

Cars

Cars symbolize our soul. What we have to notice is if we are the drivers of our soul or we let others drive. There's no such thing as good and bad. The explanation is different from person to person. We should have control over our lives and not let others take us wherever they want. We must know our destination and count on our abilities that we are able to follow my dreams. However, sometimes as year pass, we ought to let others take control let's say, trust my kids to continue my business. If I reach the age of retirement and believe that I am the only one who is able to run the business, I must realize that big ego is here again.

Tight dress

If in your dream you are wearing a tight dress that you can barely walk, it means that some situations suppress you and you can't move forwards. Think of what you are going through and find out how you can get rid of this oppressing state so as to liberate yourself and move freely.

Water

Water symbolizes sentiments. Even in real life sentimental people drink more water than people who use their thoughts more. What we should do in order to discover more about us is to observe and combine information. If you dream of deep bottomless lakes, it reveals the unconscious part of our brain which is not seen but inside it is full of life, regardless of the calm surface. Nobody can explain your dream better than you. You know if you swam or not, if you liked it or not and any other detail could lead you to understand the secret message sent to you by your inner you.

Chase- Run

If you dream of people chasing you or treat you badly, it is the power of the guardian to intercept our subconscious mind. It may hide anything that you were taught it is forbidden. All our morals and accepted behaviors were passed on us over the years. In fact, it is what pleases us more but we dare not accept let alone experience it.

Whether we remember our dreams or not it serves its purpose. When we remember them, the result comes quicker as there is more energy. That's why we tend to construct energy houses. We don't want to lose energy. Let's not choose to upgrade my house and not myself. Anxiety and stress have to do with this guardian so as to push back anything our conscious mind may not stand.

We regard it as bad because if our conscious part stands to face it then the other part will lose its throne and its kingdom. What we have to understand is that both parts are our own parts. Let's stop thinking they are sworn enemies. No, they aren't. We are responsible to introduce one another, unite them and show them the way to cooperate aligned.

Our brain tries to unite bit by bit every piece of information available in order to complete the puzzle and admire the great picture. Evolution means connecting events that are ostensibly unconnected while they were very evident in front of us. Connect facts, events, what you hear what you see and you will gradually achieve to find the relation of seemingly different things.

Christ spoke with parables. Parables are found in mathematics too. Read and compare the information you get. Since we were young we are taught of parables but nobody explained to us why. Well, in very simple words, a parable in mathematics is a U-shaped symbol where every energy beam enters goes straight to the focal point in the middle. That's why, Christ preached by using parables. His words hit our center in order to touch the essence of our heart. Parables find applications from telescopes to suspended bridges and of course this is not a random event either. We have also seen this U shape in the circle of life. Neither this is accidental. Connecting information leads you to answers your soul seeks. Unite the parts that constitute us and your life will change to the best. Work with yourself upgrade yourself, treat yourself tenderly, do not scare your inner part and solutions will transform you and your life.

Of course interpreting dreams is not an easy and univocal procedure. We must learn why all these symbols appear while I am sleeping. We have to unite information of all fields, history, mythology, etymology, religion and any other kind of information the library of my unconscious mind includes even though I am not aware of their existence. When our mind gets used to training it will act in the automate mode.

Esotericism

Our life is a circle since time is circular and we have to understand that everything on this universe moves in a circular orbit. Although all these are proven facts, we insist on believing our life is linear. This is because we have access only to a small part of this cosmic circle. Imagine a circle and try to draw a line on its perimeter. You will have to enlarge it quite a lot in order to get a little straight line. This line though, is an illusion because it just a small part of a greater circular shape. It depends on us how far we want to explore of ourselves. There are circles of various sizes and it is up to us to decide whether we want to remain trapped in the circle we are, or move upwards and find ourselves in a new event horizon.

From up here you will be able to see the vanity and fallacy you used to live and realize that every time you thought you were helpless was a new chance to move you upwards. Now you are able to secure your inner self so as no poisonous arrows can reach and affect you. You know how to protect the whole of you; you know how important it is to respect and love every part of you. Now you can trust and rely on your powers and appreciate our Creator for all you have.

Now you have managed to get out of the vicious circle that looks like the snake biting its own snake and you have the chance to breath and live free of fixed beliefs others have imposed on you in a larger circle. Enjoy the new and breathtaking view from the window you have just opened.

Now energy in your battery is more balanced and you know how to seal it in order not to lose energy out of egoism. This higher level of energy will help you enjoy your life; head towards your purpose, feel grateful for all you are and welcome every new change. Changes are no longer problems, but precious chances.

As you have managed to break the chains of the dipoles that kept you stagnant you can realize that you are part of a greater entity called humanity. You must respect the orbits and suns of every smaller entity which constitutes humanity and realize that everyone has a certain role to play. Your sun adds to the light of humanity but it is not the only one. No, that's your ego's belief. You have the potential to transmit your rays and be one of the brightest sources of light. If you look at the sky your attention is attracted by the brightest ones and you don't try to find those which are barely seen. The same thing happens here too. Every one of us sends light. Be the brighter star and attract the attentions of the cosmic energy. It is the same law upside down.

The first realization is that we an integral part of humanity, which constitutes a greater part called Earth including everything there is on it. Proportionally, Earth is a part of a greater entity called solar system, galaxy and this proportion can go on so far as our imagination can perceive. When you realize that every part that exists in this infinite universe is valuable, helpful and essential to this cosmic evolution that it is of crucial importance to turn your attention to self-realization and self- improvement, then, you have managed to kick your ego out of your house.

Now you are open to enjoy this divine power and make use of it and help the great entity we belong to evolve. You must stop thinking that you are a small unimportant particle that has nothing to offer. You value the most and do you know why? Because every invisible part of you plays a major role to your existence. Every cell works hard so that it does everything it can to keep you healthy, even though you are not conscious of that. You don't have conscience to the cells of your nails but they are there, working nonstop for you. And a time comes where you need to cut off your nail. You are not sad, but glad. You don't worry because you know it will continue to do its job undistracted and faithfully. Your conscience will be attracted if your nail makes you suffer from let's say fungi. Then it attracts your attention, just to remind you that it is there and needs your care. If your nail gives you hard times then you start appreciating it.

As we can see, nothing that exists is superfluous and unneeded. Our conscience cannot perceive smaller entities usefulness. This doesn't mean they don't exist or they are unused. Our physiology can perceive a certain spectrum of colors, mass volume, energy many other particles that constitute the world. Let's work all together to acquire as much conscience we can to be an active and necessary part of the greatest entity we belong to, even though we can't perceive. Neither the cell of our nail can perceive that there are cells on my heart too, but that doesn't stop it from working and evolving. Everything is under the same proportional law. The energy that reaches us and many times it affects our mood and the state of our nerves is difficult to explain as we lack the tools to explore everything on the universe, but that doesn't prevent us from seeing the proportion to the extend we are able to understand.

Greater and unknown systems, black holes, gravitational fields and many other unseen entities send energy to the planets we can perceive. The energy is polarized there and it is up to our evolution if we can endure it or not. The analogy of the planets on our solar system is our energy centers or endocrine glands. I have to mention again that the etymology of this Greek word means endo means *in* and ecrino means *secrete.* In other words something is inserted in us. Believe when I say that Greek language can interpret every secret meaning of life. Well, endocrine glands receive and store the cosmic energy which allows us to move. Under the same law, your organism needs vitamins.

Now imagine that I am the sun and my chakras are the planets. They exist on ether of my solar system and not on its visible mass. Accordingly, our chakras are on our ether body, our aura and not on the physical body I can see and touch. Their respond on our physical body occurs in the endocrine glands. Likewise, every single entity has its own aura, every one of us has our own solar system and our own aura. It is simple to understand if we realize that we don't need to touch the sun in order to accept its heat and effect because we can receive its aura.

You can name this aura as you wish. Whether you call it magnetic or electric or cosmic it does and transmits what it was created to do. Now, we can understand that we live on the aura of our sun. But it is not only this aura that affects us, as everything is united and we accept waves from everything that exists. This includes not only far away star systems but the aura of every person around us. Since the greater entity has everything united, we are also united. We are able not only to receive but give off energy too. It is the maypole we mentioned above that unites us all.

We can see how we transmit this energy aura to people and pets living around us. This is the way you affect your pet or receive and transmit love. There is no need to touch you in order to feel your sentiments. What our physiology lacks is the explanation of how we transmit this energy. It is the same inability to explain someone what the process you make inside you is that urges you to get up and drink water.

We tend to think that we know what we do, but unfortunately there is very little knowledge of our nature. While I cannot understand the mechanism that makes everything work perfect in me I tend to take it for granted. This way I am not am able to acquire the conscience needed. We need to work hard towards this direction and make our movements, our action and reactions, our thoughts and words as conscientious as possible. This is the only way to unlock the big window that hides the bigger picture.

We tend to believe that we know what we do and when things do not go as we want, we call it bad and we tend to blame Zeus or Hermes instead of turning my thought inside me and see my mistaken belief. We have to realize that every problem arises only when we place it on our way. That's why all people face different problems. It is easier to ignore what this energy sent to us is than to work towards the solution. We avoid trying to find our mistake because our ego tells us that we are the best. I heard that from my mum when I was five, and her sentiments blurred the truth, prevented her from being objective. Her ego led her believe that she is the only capable one of giving birth to the best aspect of her continuation.

It is up to our entity's advancement how we respond to the cosmic energy send to Earth and that's why some people have a bad day, others a good one and some are able to fully enjoy their every single day. We don't realize the way it happens. One may say that something good happened to her meaning having a new boyfriend. Another may say that something bad happened to her, meaning breaking up with a boyfriend. Who told you what is good and bad? There is an exception in the case he abuses her, that's completely different. Who defined the dipole good- bad according to a boyfriend? Only you! And do you know why? Because you are not fully conscious of the energy, you can't recognize what the lesson given to you is. As long as you don't learn the lesson, you are going to name events as good and bad.

Let's see it from an astrological aspect. Saturn is a planet that many people are afraid of mainly because it much bigger than us. He is a teacher. We belong to the ether body of the planets the same way our cells belong to us. We have cells in our stomach, in our heart, in our toes. Every cell does its job without realizing that there are also cells in my eye. That does not prevent them from working and what we have to conceive is that they are all different but necessary. We can't differentiate them and classify the cells of my heart as good and the cells of my stomach as bad. Well, Saturn controls that evolutionary part where you have the choice to undertake the responsibility or refuse to do so. It regulates whether you accept or reject the chance. It brings you before the problem and now you must decide with absolute and pure conscience how you choose to proceed. Whether you accept your responsibility or decline the obligation, you will get the respective results as well. We have already analyzed it with words and actions. Your purpose (preposition), defines your action (verb) and take the analogous result (suffix).

Now it s time you decided how you would like to step further on and your action will bring you before the responding result. Most people choose to reject responsibility. It is easier to say that it is my mum's, my kid's or my boss's fault. This way I feel fine with myself but I am not ready to suffer the consequences and define a new boyfriend as good or a separation as bad. If you don't like the result, it is not the Saturn's problem. It is the fact that you haven't decided consciously and you haven't been ready to accept that separation is a part of the game.

The only thing for sure is that every person that comes to our life is teacher. He has to teach us something and not to punish or give us hard times. It is up to us to identify the lesson I have to learn or my ego leads me to consider it as positive or negative. At first, this procedure lacks conscience by both parts until you are not stuck to sentiment or egoism but have a look at the internal lesson.

Let's approach our evolution from the chakras point of view. A very short and simple explanation will make us understand our response to the energy we receive. So, there are seven energy centers, seven chakras on our ether body. They are those who receive the energy. Our ether body is the receptor of cosmic rays. Imagine seven lights which receive energy from the ether field and this way they move our body. This signal is sent automatically, we don't control who sends me the energy. The corresponding agents in the analogy of our physical body are our endocrine glands. The seven power centers on our ether body are:

- The root chakra which is based on the base of our spine which regulates our movement.
- The sacral chakra above the pubic or holy bone which has to do with sexuality.
- The solar plexus chakra in our stomach which is related to our sentiments. That's why when we are in love we feel butterflies in the stomach.
- The fourth chakra is called heart chakra and adjusts the energy of love. It is in the middle of our chest.
- The fifth one is called Throat chakra, in our throat and is related with what we say, the way we communicate. Don't forget that by saying negative things or gossiping we lose an essential part of our energy.
- The sixth one is between our eyes. You may have heard of it as third eye or hypophysis and it has to do with our intuition.
- The top one, which is on the cortex of our brain is called Crown chakra and is related to our spiritual connection with ourselves. It is the pineal gland or epiphysis.

Planets or energy affect the three bottom chakras, that is, the root, sacral and solar one. These three accept the powers of the universe. The upper ones electroplate the three lower ones. What is asked is to elevate the energy on the upper chakras in order the three lower to be affected by upper ones and not the energy planets send down. In other words, we need to use the cosmic energy without being affected. That's why our chakras should not be blocked by negativity.

People who have managed to open the Crown chakra lit up and this is symbolized by the halo. In other words, this energy centre is so bright that the whole head is in light. It lights up there and regulates the lower chakras. That's why holy people do not care about sex or food. They are not attracted by the lower chakras. The gap is huge. In other words it is completely different to approach someone because of sexual attraction and completely different to approach someone out of love. The latter contact will give sex a more essential meaning.

It is of crucial importance to reach the point where the upper chakras regulate the lower ones. It is important to use our mind, our thought, our spirituality in order to adjust the lower ones. We all have these lights and we need to turn on as many lights as possible. Different planets affect different lights, but what is asked by us is to have the power to activate them and not feel adrift and get carried away by the mood of the planets.

Let's see it from a practical look. Suppose you want to start a new job. If you work and the sentimental part of you prevails, you are not going to get the most of it. Whatever job and idea you serve, you will suffer loss. If you start a business with someone just because he is a good man, you will both face failure. Proper judgment and sensibility are required. You have to think what the other person's target is. If his target is to make money and your target is to become popular, you can't work together. Your aims are totally different and cooperation cannot be built upon feelings just because he is an open-hearted person.

If I am a fortune hunter, my target is not to cover you sentimentally, nor am I attracted by your beauty or your temperament but your money. As a result this marriage will end up to a sinking ship because our aims were not aligned. Your sentimental state blurred the real image and you did not use your logical thought. You had all the signs of my character in front of your eyes but you were not able to see them as your solar plexus is activated and did not use a rational way of thinking. That's why you are hurt now. You were not able to realize that one plus one equals two and not three as you estimated. And I am going to ask you, so what? You should be able to see the collateral beauty and not flirt with pain. Your lesson was to learn and know you know. If you aren't a good student and fail to pass these exams, you are going to sit the test again and maybe again, until you learn. Until you learn to recognize money hunters, or whatever you have misunderstood.

Every facet of life tells the same thing. Suppose you have a spermatic idea you want to bear the best results. It is the same as in pregnancy. First is the sperm. In order the idea to be born like a baby you need to get rid of the water which symbolizes sentiments. Just like water that has to break when the amnion ruptures. The same happens with every new idea. Thought has to break sentiments otherwise spermatic ideas cannot be born.

Bear in mind that when the sound of appearance sounds louder than that of spirit then you are attracted by the appearance. When the sound of spirit sounds louder than appearance, separation from essence is unavoidable and it dies. The spirit is not attracted by the look or physical body and it continues its journey freely. This can be interpreted in many aspects but you can easily realize it in your every day relations.

In order to realize that there are no random events let's take a look at grammar rules. Verbs have grammatical moods. We have moods as well, right? Let's analyze them a bit more and understand what we express when we talk. One grammatical mood is the indicative mood where the speaker indicates the action and it sounds factual. For example "he writes a letter" or "he is writing a letter".

Another mood is the subjunctive mood directly related to the verb subjugates or in other words dominate or control. For example, "I suggest that he write a letter". In other words when I use this mood I try to dominate or take control others.

Another mood is imperative mood which commands others and it many cases it is regarded a rude way to talk. For example "Write a letter" or "Don't write a letter"

There is also the optative mood which tends to disappear and there is no use in many languages. It expresses wish and potentiality. And now I want to ask why can't a mood that expresses wishes find application in many languages?

This small sample of what language tells us is to avoid subjunctive and imperative especially when we raise kids. And I mention kids just because they are our easiest target. Our ego does not let us understand what we say but the meaning of our words and mood is transmitted. Limits cannot be commanded and nobody likes being dominated. Kids do not learn by words but they copy actions. Actions speak louder than words as the saying goes.

There are secret meanings everywhere and this internal meaning is what we should discover by combining every kind of information that we take no notice of. Whichever field you examine you are going to discover information you can connect and find internal explanations. Words hide meanings and fortunately there is etymology to help us find the hidden meanings. It is noteworthy that the word mood in Greek is engklisi which means *internal calling*. Plato tried to find out and explain Greek words since around 480 BC. How was this language created? It definitely hides great amount of wisdom and it is not an accidental event. Let's hope the truth is revealed soon.

Another fact that should not go unnoticed is that of free time. Your life is full of obligations and you barely have spare time to devote to your inner peace. Whether it is your boss or mum or even your belief you are on the go and you think that time is less than you need. Is that possible? As we have said time is circular and it is unlimited. It hasn't finished for millions of centuries. The conventions you burden yourself with act as barriers and you are able to see only a small straight line of time and you call it a day, a month or year. If you name it a life time then you have just chosen to be a loser. A loser of that great gift you were given and a loser of the chance you got to fulfill your purpose. In other words you decline to undertake the responsibility of your own evolution and by extension of humanities evolution. Don't forget that only those who train hard and compete are awarded prizes.

The problem is when you have misunderstood your mission and train for others' purpose. It sounds weird but think of how much time you have left to do what pleases your soul. That may include reading, watching a movie, painting, writing whatever. There is always an excuse to avoid these recreational activities and you look for tasks that are of no real essence. This is a misunderstood belief that others led you to consider part of your life.

You are not really to blame until you find out the inner force that makes you work like a well oiled machine. You are constantly bombarded that prices go up and you automatically try to think of ways to make more money, so your mind gives you the order that you must not stop trying. You hear everywhere that unemployment is on the rise and your mind again tunes you to be subjective to your boss or superiors. What you haven't understood is that you are able to do a certain amount of creative work. However fast or hard they order you to work, your efficiency is limited and is aligned to your skills. The excessive pressure just makes you delay but your mind believes that you are productive. The rest of the time you occupy your brain with fear and illogical hypotheses. Do you know why? The reason is simple. Fear has undertaken the wheel of your life. This fear has to do with material things. That's fine if you consider them so necessary so as to sacrifice your soul's pleasure.

The importance of this inner peace of mind is not revealed. They never inform you when some prices go down. This is because you must never neglect this endless race. You have to realize that more and more work leads to the result that there is no free time to devote to my brain work and find out the beauties of my inner world. Pressure can never be innovated and productive. How can you love anything out of stress? Suppose someone forced you to do your hobby under pressure and ordered you not to stop in order to take reviving breaths. Would you still love doing it after some time? I don't think so. And do you know why? Because any spiritual part of your pastime will be lost and this pressure is the abettor. Not only will you hate it but you will do anything to avoid doing it. From a spiritual revival and pneumatic recreation it has been grounded to an oppressive activity. Let alone allowing others to tell you how to do it. They have devastated you and you had no time to react or think twice.

You are constantly forced to think only of materialism. You try to gain fame status, money and you lose valuable time from your kids, friends, your own youth and life. This is quite a dangerous part because if people had the ample time they needed to indulge themselves, nobody would like to work. That is when inner balance is needed. Dipoles have a balance midpoint and you have to find it. Money and power is like breathing. You need as much air as your lungs, can handle. The word lungs in Greek is pneumons meaning *spirit*. It is not easy to break the materialism circle as your kids will always ask for state of the art gadgets and you will try to make them falsely happy. You will always search for saving-laboring devices that cost a lot, but in the end you will realize that you didn't actually saved time.

Not everyone is the same because everybody has his own experiences, interests, a different purpose and a different route. What we all have in common is the Awakener we hide inside us. This Awakener of ours will help us realize why we do all we do and help us find the midpoint in order to be in balance.

Have you ever wondered what the inner meaning of your job is? Whether you became a civil engineer just because you wanted to take after your dad, or because you like designing buildings, the inner part of your occupation tells much more. There is an inner psychological explanation and let's analyze it. A civil engineer builds houses. In other words he implements buildings. What else does he realize? He transforms your mental or spiritual desires into material reality.

We can take it a bit further on. It is the training to materialize earthy desires in order to advance and be able to fulfill spiritual desires. A mechanic cannot leave a building half- built. In other words, he must finish things. A cemented uninhabitable building is not attractive to anybody. So his inner purpose is to finish things. But don't forget that he must finish things with very specific ingredients and materials. He cannot replace iron with wood? If he does it, the building will not be steady and it is a matter of time to fall down.

As we can see, the internal part exists everywhere. What we have to do is acquire conscience and find this fine balance point in order not to be polarized to dipoles. This consciousness requires work but this is your inner work necessary to reach self-realization. It has nothing to do with working all day for a new model of any material thing.

Every occupation has a hidden inner purpose and if we want to elevate spiritually we have to discover it. At this lever there are no higher or lower class jobs. Everyone has his own destiny and only after he realizes it, he will stop blaming his fate. The objective you have to discover is that your job shows your purpose. If you, out of vanity, are jealous of other people's purpose, it is only your own problem and has nothing to do with others. You are standing on a seesaw alone and you think you can find harmony and enjoy it. Again, it is a matter of time to realize it and learn that this is not the correct way to use it. My advice should be to remember this flexibility step we have mentioned above and change your action. If you reject to help yourself and by extension help humanity, just because you do not understand, it is like sitting exams without studying. Why do you feel guilty if you fail? Everything you had to study was in front of you but you chose the easy way, cheating. Never mind, after some time you may retake the same exams and if you work harder you have good chances of passing and elevate to a higher level.

Every day you have two choices. The first one is to enjoy and make the most of it and the second is to curse your fate for what you have to do. The choice is absolutely yours. You are the designer of you every day and your life. Don't forget the law of attraction and repulsion. It is always there, unseen but present. If for example you wake up and realize that your coffee machine is out of order, the most possible reaction of yours is start nagging or even swearing. It has nothing to do with your luck or fate. All machines break down. If, however, cannot see it as a real fact, and a simple incident becomes uncontrollable and start saying how unlucky you are, that nothing goes right, that someone has put a curse on you, wait for them to happen. Words come back as we have said and you have forgotten it.

Do not waste all your energy to the broken coffee machine because you are going to find the elevator out of order too and if you continue blaming your fate be ready to change the flat tire on your way too. You asked for it, and it is given to you. The law of action and reaction works perfectly either you like it or not, agree or disagree, remember or forget it, see it as good or bad. You have asked for and if you are not conscious of what you ask for you are going to name it bad luck. The sooner you realize your hidden power the sooner you will be able to realize your dreams.

Nobody wants a flat tire during a busy day. The inner realization we have to make is accepting the upper will, regardless of the fact that it doesn't suit us. Of course all things break down but the point is to understand that there is a higher force which is more powerful that ours. It is mere egoism to believe that things should come as it suits us. And now we have to choose: will we accept the higher power that governs us or will we remain stagnant and insist on our vain will? This is the secret of advancing. The golden rule is to be able to accept and follow the higher will even if it is against ours. Only then will we be able to approach the higher chakras, self-realization, inner peace, and make use of the extra energy we have gathered.

This law of periodicity is what brings us before the same conditions again and again until we learn. The circle of relationships lasts about seven years. That's why seven years and by extension fourteen and so on, in marriage is regarded as a nodal point. This circle brings you back all the problems you left unsolved. If it hurts you, you will have to find the solution yourself. Nobody else can tell you what to do. You are the only one who should take on the responsibility of your actions, so as the reaction will be all yours. Either good or bad. You name it.

The ten year circle has to do with your mental understanding. It is pointless to expect to solve your inner disputes by doing nothing. This is your homework. Beware of what you ask and work towards conscientious wishes. And every circle you break you enter a new one, a bigger one and you advance. Only then, by realization will you be able to appreciate every obstacle you think it is unachievable.

This is the reason we are attracted by appearance at first, and most times by the opposite. As our mentality becomes more conscious we are attracted by the mindset and spirituality of others. It is when the sound of the soul is louder than that of the appearance. The course of action we have to follow is stopping telling lies to ourselves out of the belief that nobody will find out. Our circle will force us face it not out of vengeance but because we must learn. Our truth should be our real truth and not the ostensible truth I wish to show.

We rely on others to get us out of trouble. This happened with my mum when I was a kid. I don't need a teacher now. I can be my own instructor and face my own difficulties. If I solve them I can go on undisturbed. Nothing can interrupt me then from reaching the highness of my soul. Now, the midpoint I tried to balance is above the straight line I used to stand and the poles and my balance point form my triangle, my trinity. This in my holy trinity and I owe to respect, believe and trust it.

Conclusion

To conclude this inner journey I want to remind you that everything that happens to you, everything you see and everything you hear concern you and only you. What you need to do is realize what secret meaning they want to send you. Your subconscious mind gives you a cheat sheet to help you pass the exams and the only one who can stop you from getting this information is your conscious mind because it does not understand what it is. Love yourself, respect any secret desire of your soul, trust your inner forces, and find your hidden power inside you.

There is nothing more worthy than discovering who you really are, how powerful you are and how sophisticatedly created you are. Everything you need to know is in front of you. You have just to start connecting the puzzle in order to reveal the big picture. This big picture will automatically convert your thoughts, actions and reactions. You have advanced now and minor problems are easy to solve. You are no longer the person who wandered aimlessly. Now you know what you have to do and how to do it.

What we have difficulty in understanding is that we were divinely sent to this world and our soul feels imprisoned as we are told what to do for many years and sometimes for our whole life. You have no power to raise your head and see the magnitude of cosmic freedom. That is over now. You are a grown up and you can open the door which is in front of you. It is not a boundary, it is your redemption. However, if you still face a wall you can always draw your own door and let you free. Let your soul express your inner needs and feel in harmony with the cosmic energy and try to absorb all the love which is sent by our Creator. Feel blessed and thank Him for all you have. Realize that everything you have gone through led you to love yourself. They were the necessary ingredients to transform you into who you are now. Even Hercules went through twelve Labors. That made him superior and unique. We are under the same physical laws and inhabit in the same cosmic circles. Until we break them and advance we are going to receive everything that takes us out of our comfort zone as an obstacle and bad luck. This is the way we are tuned. If you tune our minds that these hurdles lead us to open opportunities and grab them consciously, then you are ready to enjoy the privilege of loving yourself.

It is a good idea to close your eyes and talk to the little child hidden inside you. Go back and talk to you when you were at the age of two. Be tender and kind. Ask from your baby self to have faith and although your way is not going to be smooth and stable, you are going to be the winner. This is the way to be a champion. Every champion experiences defeats and only by hard training do they manage to break their record. Confirm your little self that atonement is your destination and you will do everything not to lose time and energy. This chat with your inner two year self really helps you reassure yourself that you do your best to keep you happy. Remind yourself that you love you and you will be faithful to this love affair forever.

At this point I would also like to note that the word trust in Greek is empistosyni which means *have faith in me.* This truth is so great because we have learnt that others are worthy of our trust more than ourselves. This is a misunderstood belief you have to reassess. Who else deserves your faith more than you? Who else knows your inner urges more than you? Who else can harmonize with your soul more than you? Who else is more faithful to you than you? Who else can be you or better who else do you permit to be you? No other person has the same imprint on this world as you as no one else has the same hand writing or fingerprint as you. Believe in you, and let love penetrate in your every single cell. Then you can transform into love and be a carrier of this healing energy.

Another thing you should never forget in order to be aligned with your soul is to close your inner door against intruders. Do not let people who step on your unsteady sentimental state and manipulate you. Only if you really know who you are will you feel safe with you. Others may ask whatever they want but do not forget that you have the right to decide what you want. Never deceive others but don't forget that you must not choose to deceive yourself either.

Think of lifeguards trying to save a drowning person. The person in danger is so strong that he can drag down to the bottom everyone who catches him. Lifeguards throw a rescue can in order to save others and not put themselves in danger too. This is the right technique to save others without hurting ourselves. Do not get involved sentimentally because they can drag you to the bottom. Use your logic thought in order to save him and keep yourself intact. This is the right way to help them and if they are hurt, you have achieved to help them realize their own misunderstood beliefs. Your logic course of action helps them catch their life jacket and swim to their sandy beach. The same applies when a baby hurts his knees. He cries but you are not involved in his sentiment and cry by his side for hours. You use your logic thought and react immediately by treating his wood.

Every aspect of our life gives you the right tactic to be and love yourself. Connect situations and step by step you are going to get out of the underground passage you feel trapped. Stand up and start moving on. Remove any obstacle and have faith to our Creator. We are given part of His star dust and it is a pity to keep it locked and buried. Get to the top, let brightness and love touch you, breathe freely, feel blessed and be a part of this infinite life bearing light. Realize your strength and make use of it. You owe it to your soul.

Your uniqueness is a piece of the big puzzle. Don't tear yourself, don't abuse yourself. Humanity needs you in order to be completed and your soul knows exactly what you were born for. Listen to your inner self, appreciate the whole of you, follow your initial imprint and love your every single particle of you. Love is on the way. Welcome it, enjoy its company, treat it with care and absorb as much as possible of this healing and therapeutic energy. Now you are love, you shine and nothing can block this divine glow.

About the Author

Kiki Tsiridou was born in the town of Drama in Northern Greece. She studied in England and moved back to Greece where she has her own private school. She is a translator and script writer as well. She has studied analytical graphology , decoding dreams,inner astrology and symbols. She continued her studies as a life coach and she is a Senior Professional member of the Hellenic Institute for Coaches. Her passion to spread all this combined knowledge created this book as an attempt to make people respect, appreciate and love themselves. It is time we stopped avoiding to face our hidden inner power.

Printed in the United States
by Baker & Taylor Publisher Services